JUST FOR A MOMENT, I SAW THE LIGHT

JUST FOR A MOMENT I SAW THE LIGHT

JOHN DUCKWORTH

VICTOR BOOKS

A DIVISION OF SCRIPTURE PRESS PUBLICATIONS INC.
USA CANADA ENGLAND

The stories in this book are true. A few names have been changed
to protect the identities of those involved.

Unless otherwise noted, all Scripture references are from
the *Holy Bible, New International Version®*. Copyright © 1973,
1978, 1984 by International Bible Society. Used by permission
of Zondervan Publishing House. All rights reserved.
Other quotes are from the *New American Standard Bible* (NASB),
© the Lockman Foundation 1960, 1962, 1963, 1968, 1971,
1972, 1973, 1975, 1977; and the *Revised Standard Version
of the Bible* (RSV), © 1946, 1952, 1971, 1973.

Copyediting: Barbara Williams
Cover Design: Scott Rattray
Cover Photo: Index Stock

Library of Congress Cataloging-in-Publication Data

Duckworth, John (John L.)
    Just for a moment, I saw the light / by John Duckworth.
        p.   cm.
    ISBN 1-56476-307-2
    1. Duckworth, John (John L.)   2. Christian biography—
United States. 3. Christian life—Anecdotes. I. Title.
    BR1725.D716A3 1994
    277.3′082′092—dc20
[B]   93-49886
                                                       CIP

---

1 2 3 4 5 6 7 8 9 10 Printing/Year 98 97 96 95 94

Contents

Dedication

To Katherine, who lives in the Light

Introduction

Why should you want to read about things that have happened to me?

I can't think of a single reason — unless we have a lot in common.

And we do, you and I.

We both spend a lot of time fumbling around in the dark.

That's because we live on a planet where the fuses have blown, where the circuit breakers have snapped, where the lights have gone out. It happened long before we got here, when Adam and Eve refused to follow the power company's rules. Since then, we've all been knocking into each other and wondering what things would look like if only we could see.

Sometimes the light comes on, if just for a moment. It may flare harshly as lightning or glow subtly as a lightning bug. The Father of Lights doesn't need much time or candlepower to remind us that

He's still there, that His Word is still true, that He still loves us. He uses all kinds of things — chance remarks, irritations, encounters with strangers, jokes, tragedies — to illuminate those truths. Until we see the Light in person, these brief bursts are all we have, or need.

This is a book about light — bright flashes, steady beacons, tiny sparks. It's a collection of true stories about how the light has sometimes broken through for me. It's an admission that, having seen, I often correct my path for just a moment — then wander off the track again.

Perhaps that's something else you and I have in common.

Maybe that's the best reason to read this book.

The important thing is not that I've seen the Light, but that you've seen it — and that you'll see it again. I hope these stories shimmer some for you, and help to get your eyes accustomed to seeing all the glints and glimmers God plans to send your way.

Beginners

IT WASN'T *MY* IDEA TO SEE THE LIGHT.

It was all my father's doing.

Not that I was an atheist, a skeptic, or devoted to another faith. It was just that I was three years old, and the Light was pretty scary.

That well-lit room scared me, anyway. It was full of bright colors and chattering children, none of whom I'd seen before. That was reason enough to run.

So when my father tried to deposit me for the first time in Mrs. Loeffler's Sunday School class for beginners at the First Presbyterian Church of Flushing, New York, I resisted. Towering strangers tried to coax me toward a little seat in a sea of little seats, but I knew that was no place for me. Whirling, I stumbled blindly toward my father, who was trying in vain to tiptoe from the room. I wrapped my chubby arms around his legs and wailed.

He must have looked helpless, because Mrs. Loeffler herself had to come to his rescue.

"Why don't you stand in the back of the room?" she suggested to him.

So he did, trying to look reassuring as I was led away. Eventually he sat down.

I sat on a much smaller chair, checking and re-checking over my shoulder to make sure he was still there. All around me were the old hands, the preschoolers who knew what was going on. They knew the songs and the motions, and they knew what was about to happen when Mrs. Loeffler carefully placed a set of paper people on her flannelboard at the front of the room. It was story time.

Perhaps the Bible story that day was about Zaccheus, the little paper man who slid up the paper tree to see someone named Jesus. Maybe Mrs. Loeffler led the class in singing about the wee little man and showed us how to claw at that sycamore tree and shade our eyes like sea captains so that we could peer over the crowd, the Savior for to see.

But whether it was Zaccheus, or David and Goliath, or Noah, it was all new to me. I could have taught the class all about Santa Claus and the intricacies of leaving a plateful of cookies on Christmas Eve and listening for the sleigh bells and eight tiny reindeer, but Bible stories were *terra incognita*.

I had never seen the Light, not even a glint or a glow.

So when Mrs. Loeffler stage-managed her cutout characters across that flannelboard, I watched. I listened, my fears fading for a moment, and wondered.

And in the back of the room, unknown to me or to Mrs. Loeffler or to anyone but God Himself, someone else was watching and wondering. It was a dark-haired, thirty-year-old man who sat on a chair because his little boy would not let him leave. It was my father, who like me knew all about Santa Claus, but nothing of Zaccheus or Moses or Adam and Eve.

He had never seen the Light, not even a spark or a glimmer. To other grown-ups he called himself an agnostic, and had come to church only to please his wife and because Sunday School might somehow be a good influence on his son.

So there we were, my father and I, both of us beginners. We were locked in a roomful of light with
no escape, the son trapped by the father and the
father by the son.

We had come to the right place.

The following week we came back. Still unwill-
ing to stay without my father, I made sure he found
his spot in the back of the room. Mrs. Loeffler ar-
ranged her paper people on the flannelboard, and
again the Light began to shine.

For the next six weeks it shone as Mrs. Loeffler
and her flannel-backed figures told the stories my
father and I had never heard. Goliath marched
across the flannel, taunting the boyish David, who
knocked him flat with a stone and the power of a
God we had never met. Adam and Eve hid modest-
ly in the paper bushes, freshly formed by the same
God, suddenly barred from their garden home by
their wrongdoing — and by a paper angel with a
flaming sword.

The Light shone on all of us, but its warmth was
felt most deeply by the man in the back of
the room. It was not supposed to work this way,
that a grown man, a man ten times the age of most
of us in the class, would watch so intently. But it

did, and as it did something began to happen in that man's grown-up heart.

It happened most profoundly the week Mrs. Loeffler told the special story, the one about God's love. Something more than paper and flannel was at work as Mrs. Loeffler revealed the amazing news: God had sent His Son, Jesus, to save people. To save everybody who would believe in Him — thirty-year-old fathers, three-year-old sons. Jesus had died for us, and then had come back to life so that we could live forever.

Sin, death, resurrection, heaven — the Light was too bright for a three-year-old, and most of us in the room were mentally squinting. But far in the back a man was beginning to see.

He had started to hear pieces of this special story, first from his wife who had heard it as she'd grown up, and then from some men of the church who had come to visit. But it had never made this much sense before, had never rung true. It had never been this simple: God loving us and showing it, right there on the flannelboard. Anyone could see the innocent Jesus letting go of His life on a cross on a hill, being hidden in a gray paper tomb, and coming back to see His friends — a Mary so

15

happy she might cry at any moment, and disciples so wide-eyed they looked as if they might never calm down. Anyone could see that God had offered people a priceless present, and all we had to do was take it. It was all right there if you only looked.

My father did look, and saw, and began to believe.

It all happened silently, without any of us knowing. Even Mrs. Loeffler couldn't have known that her old, old story was so new to the man in the back of the room. She couldn't know how deeply he was touched by the simple idea that God loved him. She kept telling the story to the rest of us, moving her paper people around, unconsciously choosing her words for just the right group: the beginners of all ages.

During those six weeks my father and I heard many stories, many songs. But when the time came for Dad to leave because I had finally settled down, one story stood out in his memory. It was the story of God's love, of God sending His Son.

Four months later he was ready to act on the message he'd seen that day. He stepped fully into the Light, asking Jesus to be his Savior. He'd

learned many things about Christianity during
those four months, but none more important than
the simple fact that God loved him.

Already my mother had taken a similar step. One
year later, having seen flashes of light in people
like Mrs. Loeffler and Mom and Dad, I would walk
down the burgundy carpet of the sanctuary aisle
and give my beginner's heart to Jesus too.

Now we were all beginners together.

Not until three years later did Mrs. Loeffler finally learn all that had happened in the back of her
Sunday School room. My parents had to tell her
the story before we left town — before we drove
across the country to my father's first pastorate.
The simple story on the flannelboard had changed
the whole direction of his life, and ours.

Nearly forty years have passed since I sat in
Muriel Loeffler's class. I still remember the memory verses I learned there, the action songs, the stories of David and Goliath and Zaccheus and Adam
and Eve.

But most of all I remember the wonder of seeing
the Light for the first time.

I keep losing sight of that wonder now, and
when I do I want to go back. I want to fly back in

time to the fall of 1956, to a bright room with tiny chairs lined up at shiny tables, surrounded by cheerful bulletin boards. I want to sing "Deep and Wide" and do the motions, and slip my missionary offering dime through the slot of the church-shaped bank, and hear it go *clunk* in the bottom.

I want to see Mrs. Loeffler again, smiling and readying her envelope of Bible characters for the softly wrinkled background of the flannelboard. I want to hear her say, this time to me, "Why don't you stand in the back of the room?"

And then, older now than my father was when he stood there, I want to watch in wonder as the simplest, most essential story ever told unfolds before my widened eyes. I want to see God loving me, sending His Son to pay for my sins on a hill, bringing Him back to a surprising and happy life, for me, for me.

I want to see the Light, just the Light, for itself. For Himself.

I want to be a beginner again.

This Little Light of Mine

WITNESSING. The very word still gives me chills. It sounds like getting shots for rabies, delivering a speech when you've lost your notes, and skydiving with a defective parachute — all at the same time.

I guess my problem with it started in the fourth grade.

Perhaps I was not a normal fourth-grader. All the other kids seemed to worry about nothing more substantial than getting enough valentines, winning the science fair, and not dropping their glass-insulated thermoses on the school-bus floor. I, on the other hand, felt that I held the eternal destiny of everyone around me in the palm of my hand.

Maybe that came from being a preacher's kid,

which seemed to multiply the gravity of being a Christian to the third or fourth power. Maybe it came from reading dozens of Sunday School stories in which my fictional peers shared their faith as easily as I might share M & Ms — constantly inviting their classmates to church and never getting no for an answer.

Whatever the reason, my nine-year-old brain was gripped by an overwhelming sense of responsibility to witness — and an overwhelming sense of guilt over never having done so.

The pressure to right this wrong grew daily, until one morning I woke up knowing that this was the day I finally would witness. I had to do it — to somebody, anybody, or I would explode.

That morning at recess, I stood on the playground of Trentwood Elementary and gazed across the asphalt at the other members of the Monster Club — a loose-knit fraternity four of us boys had formed. Our goals were threefold: to talk about monsters, to pretend to be monsters, and to buy plastic model kits which, when assembled, looked like monsters.

It was not the kind of relationship that lent itself to discussing eternal truths, but it would have to do. Heart hammering in my ears, I approached freckle-faced, red-haired Jerry, the one who liked to be called Wolfman.

"I, uh, need to talk to you for a minute," I said, maneuvering him away from the others. He looked irritated as I led him around the corner of the brick school building.

I stopped. He stopped. I felt lightheaded, as if this might be a dream. We stared at each other for a long moment.

"Jerry," I asked, trying to hide the tremble in my voice, "do you know Jesus as your Savior?"

He looked at me, speechless, as though I were wearing my pants on my head. I plowed ahead anyway, pouring out all the Bible verses and unassailable proofs I had stored for so long.

Jerry just stared as I talked faster and faster to fill up the silence. Finally I reached my closing argument: "Really, it's true!"

Jerry did not do what the kids in the Sunday School stories did. He turned and walked back to the playground, shaking his head. "Hey, you guys," he called to our fellow monsters. "This guy is crazy! He's telling me about religion — trying to get me to join up or something!"

The others didn't laugh. They did something worse.

They stared at me as if I were an outsider.

And from that moment on, I was.

The Monster Club disbanded soon after that. Nobody gave a reason; we all just seemed to lose interest. At least the other three members did.

And I decided to keep quiet. Witnessing just wasn't worth it. I put a bushel over my little light and tried not to think about how bright or dark my corner of the world might be.

But as the years passed, the pressure built again. The stories in the Sunday School papers grew more insistent, warning me to witness before all the non-Christians I knew died suddenly in car accidents or avalanches. I heard that Jesus would not mention me in heaven if I didn't talk about Him on earth. By tenth grade the size of my unpaid witnessing debt seemed almost beyond repaying, and I feared my redemption was in jeopardy.

Once again I had to do my duty, clear my conscience, take a stand. But this time I would be smarter. This time I would minimize the risk, writing my message down instead of speaking it.

Carl was my new target. The stocky, bespectacled son of a farmer was the closest thing I had to a friend after just a year at Stanwood High — and our family was about to move to another state. For Carl it was now or never.

I tried to think of a way to start, some common ground he and I might share. But I couldn't think of anything. When I got right down to it, I didn't know Carl very well at all. But that didn't matter, because I had to witness to him.

Then, just as time was running out, I happened to look at the top of our refrigerator. There sat a scale model of the *U.S.S. Enterprise* from the "Star Trek" TV series, one of the few models I'd built since the demise of the Monster Club. Carl had admired it once.

That was it! I'd give Carl the model as a good-bye gift. I'd put a note in the box about my faith. Technically that would be witnessing, wouldn't it?

Dear Carl, I wrote, *There's something I haven't told you about.* . . .

I went on to vaguely describe my faith. If Carl wanted to know more, the note said, he could write me.

I waited until we were ready to leave town. Then, without knocking on the screen door or

23

ringing the doorbell, I placed the box on the cement porch of Carl's house and slipped away.

My cowardice left me ashamed.

And I never heard from Carl again.

Once more I'd learned my lesson: Witnessing wasn't worth it. If speaking up had led to embarrassment, so had the silent route. Nothing worked.

I took hold of that bushel over my little candle and nailed it down tight. If the world got a little darker, I thought, that was too bad. Everyone would just have to get used to it.

That might have been the end of the story — if not for Al.

I met Al the year I worked in a lumberyard, ten years after sneaking away from Carl's front porch. Al and I punched cash register buttons at the lumber counter. While we punched, he talked a lot — about his ex-wife, about his lawyer, about all the people who were making his life miserable. As he talked his cigarette would wag up and down, seemingly glued to his lower lip.

I listened, but didn't say much. If Al needed to hear about God, he wasn't going to hear it from me. My witnessing days were over.

One day Al's monologue sounded more somber

than usual. I listened more closely. It seemed his young son needed emergency dental work, and Al didn't have the money to pay for it.

I thought about Al's little boy off and on that afternoon. Somebody had to help; the need was so obvious. Maybe I could give Al some money. Maybe some people from the Bible study I attended could help too.

It turned out that they could. Next morning I went to work with a check in my hand.

I led Al down an aisle, away from the other employees. "Al, I've got something for you," I said. "It's for your son's dental work."

Surprised, he accepted the envelope. He looked as if the cigarette might finally fall out of his mouth.

"It's from me and my Bible study group," I added. "We're thankful because God has given us so much, and we want to share it with you."

Al tried to think of something to say. While he did I kept hearing echoes of the last sentence I'd spoken.

Had *I* said that? Words about God, to a non-Christian? Had I forgotten how risky it was to do that?

I hadn't felt pressure or pain. I wasn't embarrassed or ashamed. What was going on?

Finally Al found his voice. "I'm beginning to feel thankful too," he said. Later he handed me a note, thanking the Bible study group. "You have renewed my faith," he had written, "in people and in God."

It wasn't a conversion. But there had been a conversation. It was almost as if my little candle were starting to burn a hole in the bushel basket I'd nailed over it.

It had been too easy, I thought. *All I'd done was listen to Al, and respond to his need, and—*

His need. That was it. For once I'd forgotten my need to do my duty, to witness. I'd noticed someone else's need instead, and had done what had come naturally—helped and explained why.

Anybody could do that. Even *I* could do that. Maybe the more I tried it, the more naturally it would come.

Why had I taken so long to see it? Maybe I'd paid too much attention to stories about witnessing and too little to the Subject.

I should have known that if anyone knew how to spread Good News, it was Jesus. Looking for needs and meeting them was the way He worked— listening and asking questions, touching wounds and speaking words. He was pulled by others' needs, not pushed by guilt or fear or desperation.

He would have known what to do on that fourth-grade playground, because He would have known the things that really scared the members of the Monster Club. He would have asked.

He would have known what to do with Carl, because He would have known the needs of a sixteen-year-old farmer's son. He would have listened.

He would have known what to do with Al. And for once, almost by accident, I had done something like that too.

* * * *

I don't know where the members of the Monster Club are now. And I lost track of Carl long ago.

But if someday you should meet a red-haired guy who wants to tell you why the Wolfman could beat Frankenstein in a fight, or a stocky guy with glasses who likes to talk about tractors, I hope you'll listen.

Listen to their needs. Respond if you can. And tell them why.

You'll be doing them — and me — a big favor. You might even be . . . *witnessing.*

The Man Who Could Not Blink

WE DIDN'T GET MANY GUEST SPEAKERS or singers at the Foothills Community Church. But that's not why I remember the guest we had one Sunday when I was eight. Anybody from any church, large or small, would have remembered him.

He came even though Foothills wasn't on the lecture or concert circuit. It wasn't even on the map. It was just an area, a rural collection of grass and wheat farms and scattered houses about twenty miles from Spokane, Washington.

He lived in Spokane, where he was the minister of music in a large church. No doubt that was why he said yes when my father, pastor of the Foothills Community Church, asked him to come after hearing him sing at a luncheon.

Tonight, in the evening service, our church was going to hear the four-octave vocal range and the testimony that had so impressed my father. It would be a big night for our church.

But I didn't know that. I was not supposed to know. My parents thought it best that my younger brother and I not see the guest singer who was coming all the way from Spokane.

They thought he might scare us.

They were right.

All went as they planned until the man from Spokane drove up to the Foothills Community Church. Instead of pulling into the unpaved parking lot, he turned left and kept going. He drove past the closed-down one-room schoolhouse across the road and down into the hollow. In front of our little house, he pulled to a stop.

Perhaps my parents didn't hear his car. What ever the reason, their plan to keep us from seeing the guest soloist went awry.

When the knock came, I got to the door first.

I opened it, and there he was.

I don't remember whether he said anything. But if I thought of any words, they were strangled in my throat as I looked up. I stared at him, and tried not to stare.

The two of us seemed suspended in that door-way for a painfully long time. Eventually my par-ents stepped up, greeting our guest and inviting him in, giving up on the notion of shielding me from him.

It was too late for shielding. I had already seen his face.

It looked like a mask, this face. The skin was pulled taut over the bones, and there were almost no features. The mouth was little more than a slit; the ears were missing; the hair was sparse and started too far back on the head. The flesh looked real enough, but seemed molded together in pieces, molded badly, as if a child had tried and failed to sculpt a face out of scraps of Silly Putty. There was a fragile quality about it all, the skin thin and tender-looking like a baby's. His hands were mottled too, but mostly I saw the face.

I looked away. I took some deep breaths. I wanted to run, but I wanted to stay to find out how someone could look the way this man did. So I sat with the grown-ups in our tiny living room, listen-ing as he told his story.

His name was Merrill Womack. Until a few years before, he had looked just like anybody else. He

31

had been a singer, performing all sorts of songs—not just church music—and even recording an album or two. And on the side, he'd been a pilot.

One day he'd been flying his small plane. Something had gone wrong. The plane had lost power, dipped, and headed for the trees.

Somehow the plane had made it to the ground without breaking up. The young pilot was still alive. But then the gas tank exploded underneath him, and he was engulfed in a fireball.

When the ambulance finally got there, he was literally burned beyond recognition. His whole body was scorched, except where he was protected by his flight jacket—which, of course, did not include his face. That was swollen like a burnt marshmallow.

Through it all, he remained conscious.

The ambulance attendants didn't know how he could be alive, much less awake. Yet during the long ride to the hospital, he stayed awake by singing hymn after hymn. Doctors told him later that the singing had probably saved his life.

At the hospital the staff was stunned. Some nurses assigned to take care of him had taken one look and run out of his room.

But somehow he had survived. He no longer looked fully human, but he had survived.

At first he hadn't wanted to go out in public, much less resume his singing. But in time he tried it, and people — at least some people — had accepted him. Soon he had abandoned secular songs and was sticking with sacred ones, singing in churches and at luncheons and even on a couple of albums.

Dozens of skin grafts later, here he was. The doctors were just starting to build his ears, he said. There would be dozens more operations to come.

I sat there, taking it all in. It was an incredible story of God's sustaining power, to be sure, but it was also the kind of story to keep an eight-year-old boy riveted. It had everything — a courageous young pilot in a flight jacket, a fiery explosion, nurses afraid to look, survival against the odds.

And there was one thing more, something our guest mentioned as he described what it was like to live behind that face. It was a detail that caught my attention and would not let me go.

When the fire had engulfed him, his eyelids had burned away. As a result, he could not blink.

Now whenever his eyes watered, the liquid

would just run down his face. Often he or his wife had to dab at his face with tissues to soak up the tears.

I looked at the almond-shaped openings into which his eyes were set. Sure enough, there were no eyelids. He hoped to have some eventually, but that was many operations away.

I wondered what it was like never to be able to blink, never to close his eyes. Did he have to sleep with a blindfold over his face?

I wondered what it was like to have tears run down his face uncontrolled, and to depend on others to help him wipe them away. Did his wife usually sit next to him with a box of tissues? She was not there that day, but I imagined her to be a devoted young woman with blond hair and a pink dress, a helpmate who dabbed gently and frequently at the tears running down her husband's face.

I don't know what else was said that afternoon as we sat around the living room, trying not to gape at our guest. I don't even recall whether I went to the concert that night. All I know is that I thought about his face for a long, long time. I especially thought about his eyes.

Of all the difficulties that man had — all the scars, all the pain, all the surgeries that stretched before him — the one that fastened itself to my psyche that day and has stayed with me for over thirty years is the fact that he could not blink.

It seemed so sad not to be able to blink, not to be able to close your eyes, not to be able to stop looking unless you turned your head or covered your face. It seemed so tragic to have tears running down your cheeks without having a say in it, and to have other people drying them. It seemed so vulnerable, powerless, helpless.

Maybe that was why it bothered me so much. Vulnerable, powerless, and helpless were things I did not want to be. I wanted to shut my eyes to disturbing sights, to keep the tears contained. And I certainly did not want others to see when I had to cry, much less wait for them to take the tears away.

In that respect I haven't changed in thirty years. And I am not alone, I think.

I still reserve my right to blink. I still would rather live with facial scars than lose my power to look away, to close my eyes, to hold back tears, to dry my cheeks when I can't help but weep.

I still forget that I serve One who saw things differently. He was not a man who could not blink; He was the Man who *chose* not to.

He chose not to close His eyes to the shriveling victim of disease, the sobbing victim of loss, the sleepwalking victim of false religion. Nor did He stop His tears before they could spill over, before someone might see and say that He truly loved His friends.

His book echoes His example:

"I tell you, open your eyes and look at the fields! They are ripe for harvest" (John 4:35).

"Each of you should look not only to your own interests, but also to the interests of others" (Phil. 2:4).

"If anyone has material possessions and sees his brother in need but has no pity on him, how can the love of God be in him?" (1 John 3:17)

God has not given me permission to blink. In a spiritual sense, I lost my eyelids when I saw the Light. So did we all.

Now it is our privilege to see the things that cause others to squeeze their eyes shut, to let the tears flow because of what we see. It is also our honor to let others comfort us, to let them dry our tears, until the day when God Himself will finally wipe those tears away.

At least that's the way it's supposed to be.

As I said, we didn't get many guest singers or speakers at the Foothills Community Church.

But after Merrill Womack, I didn't need another. I'm still thinking about his eyes, trying to learn to see.

The Day the House Came Down

"THE LORD'S WORK" — that was what Dad and Mom always called it. When they talked to us kids about their roles as rural pastor and pastor's wife, they would say, "Since we entered the Lord's work . . . " or, "When you're in the Lord's work . . . "

I knew the phrase well. I saw it all the time in missionary prayer letters and heard it in speeches at our mission board's annual conference.

I also knew the phrase had to be used correctly. It was bad form to say, "I am *doing* the Lord's work"; it sounded too much like bragging. If you claimed to be doing the Lord's work, you probably weren't. The Lord's work was something you were in, like the army.

But I wasn't sure whether preachers' kids were in the Lord's work. After all, we hadn't enlisted. We didn't have to grapple with problems like hard-drinking husbands who wouldn't let their wives go to prayer meeting, offerings that were never enough, and board members who argued over the height of the new steeple. We left those things to our parents.

But we had to deal with the fallout. I, for one, was keeping a mental list of the sacrifices I was making for the Lord's work — what it was costing me to be a preacher's kid. By the time I was ten years old, the list was pretty lengthy: cramped parsonages, not being able to afford restaurant meals, having to go to church all the time, having to move so much, having visitors in the house at all hours of the day and night. . . .

The list went on and on, and grew longer all the time. Whenever my little brother Paul and I were carted off to sing a falsetto duet of "Wonderful Words of Life" at a nursing home, I added another grievance to the list. Whenever I compared my bargain-bin clothes to the latest styles the other kids wore, the list lengthened further.

Sometimes I felt like a martyr without a cause.

This "Lord's work" army I'd been drafted into didn't seem to be doing much of importance. More church services, more potlucks, more flowers in front of the pulpit — was that why I had to sacrifice so much?

Then came the day my question was answered. It was the day the house came down.

We didn't know what was happening at first. All we knew was that a fire engine had just screamed past our house. It was the volunteer fire department truck, the only emergency vehicle in the farming area where we lived near Spokane, Washington. The truck was headed toward Mt. Spokane, where the houses were even fewer and farther between.

My father jumped into his car and took off, following the siren. Like the fire truck, he was the only thing of his kind for miles. If there was a fire, the services of a pastor might be needed.

Maybe he thought he would offer comfort, or prayer, or even help the firemen haul hoses. He had done things like that before.

But not this time. As he sped up the road toward the mountain, he didn't know that he would be called upon to do far more.

When the fire truck reached its destination, it pulled up to a house and stopped. Following, Dad recognized it as the Barnett place. He had met most of the Barnett family; the wife, teenage daughter, and other children had been coming to church for a little while. Mr. Barnett had been staying home.

Dad parked behind the fire engine and got out, wondering what was going on.

There was no fire. But under the house, something terrible had happened.

Mr. Barnett had decided to put a full basement under the house. In preparation, he had jacked up the whole building on massive logs. No one was sure exactly what had gone wrong, but somehow a jack or a log had slipped. The house had collapsed, and Mr. Barnett was under it.

No one knew whether he was alive or dead. The family stood nearby, waiting, agonizing.

"Stay back from the edge! Stay back from there!" The firemen warned the bystanders; the adults warned the children. Another log, another jack might give way any second. The house could shift and crack, and someone else could be trapped.

42

Dad peered under the building. There in the dimness he could barely make out the figure of a man, hunched over, head bent to chest. There was no movement.

What if he's alive? Dad thought.

Dad wasn't sure what Mr. Barnett's relationship with God might be. What if the man was alive physically, but not spiritually? There might still be time to reach him — to communicate with him, pray with him, touch him.

Even as the possibilities spun through his mind, Dad saw another man, maybe a volunteer fireman, preparing to crawl under the house. Someone had to find out whether Mr. Barnett had survived.

Dad sank to his knees — not to pray, but to crawl under the house too.

The two men made their way slowly under the tilted structure, not knowing whether it might topple further. Five, ten, fifteen feet they crawled through the narrow passage on hands and knees, looking at the motionless figure in front of them.

Twenty feet. Twenty-five. And then there was Mr. Barnett, and at last they could see how things were, and all hope was gone. The other man felt for a pulse, but it was clear that Mr. Barnett was dead. A log lay on his back, crushing his head into his chest. He had suffocated.

There was nothing anyone could do under the house now. Dad's next thought was of the dead man's family, especially the wife and teenage daughter who waited outside. Everyone would expect the pastor to comfort them.

The lethal weight still poised over their heads, Dad and the other man crawled back into the sunlight. They broke the bad news. The daughter fainted; Dad reached out, catching her as she sank to the ground.

He stayed until other relatives came to take care of the wife and children. It wasn't until he drove home that he finally felt himself shaking.

That was the way it was when you were in the Lord's work, my father might have said. Sometimes you had to do things just because they had to be done. You didn't do them because you felt ready. You did them because they needed doing, and you depended on the Lord to help you do them.

When Dad finally made it to our house, Mom was waiting for him. She had been waiting there nervously for two hours, ever since someone had phoned to say that the Barnett house had collapsed. She didn't know what Dad might have to do, but she knew from experience that he would be in the thick of things.

That was the way it was when you were in the Lord's work, my mother might have said. Sometimes you had to wait and pray and wait some more, and accept the fact that what you were waiting for might never come. You didn't do it because it was easy. You did it because you had committed yourself a long time ago, no matter where the road might lead.

My father conducted the funeral service for Mr. Barnett. Later, after the collapsed house was torn down, Dad joined the volunteer crew that built a new home for the Barnett family. This time it had a basement. Dad helped pour the concrete floor near the spot where he had crawled not long before.

That was the way it was when you were in the Lord's work, my parents might have said. You kept giving when the official part was over, even after hours, even when it was inconvenient. You did it not because you would be rewarded, but because there were more needs than laborers.

They didn't deliver any of these lectures to me,

of course. They didn't have to, not after I learned what had happened when the house came down.

After that it was much harder to take my list of sacrifices seriously. I tried, and even added to it occasionally. But it wasn't easy when I'd seen my own father lay down his life as part of the Lord's work.

So I got used to small houses. I learned a lot of good hymns by going to church all the time. I learned to spot a bargain, and saw a lot of the country by moving around so much.

And I learned that the Lord's work included things like crawling under houses, catching the faint, waiting anxiously by the telephone, and pouring concrete. I saw that all of us, from preachers' kids to farmers to firefighters to moms, enlisted in a vast army when we met the Commander-in-Chief.

I found that we serve, not because we live in parsonages, but because we live on the front lines. A few of us get our names on the church sign; a lot of us don't.

But all of us get to have the greatest job in the world: serving the One who loves us most.

That's just the way it is when you're in the Lord's work.

A Shove from Above

I HAVE A PROBLEM.

I don't have any good miracle stories.

I don't mean the things you recognize as miracles after you think about them for a long time, like the marvels of the circulatory system or sunsets. I don't even mean grand and mysterious concepts like atonement and salvation.

I mean miracles. The obvious kind, with God reaching down and poking a hole in the natural order. I mean healings and visions and voices — the kind of thing that doesn't require a lot of reflection and guesswork and panel discussions to figure out.

Look at all those amazing events in the Bible. You don't need a master's degree to see that the parting of the Red Sea was a little unusual. You don't have to think twice about who lit the burning bush, the pillar of fire, or the flaming altar on Mt. Carmel.

Those were miracles, all of them. Bible people saw so many angelic visitations, resurrections, and bread-and-fish multiplications that they probably couldn't tell what the natural order was anymore.

But I don't have any stories like that.

Sometimes I think I'm the only one who doesn't. Once, as I rode in the back of an airport limousine, the driver asked me, "Have you heard of the See-ing-Eye-Socket Miracle?"

When I admitted that I hadn't, he explained that the son of a certain traveling evangelist had lost an eye. The miracle was that the young man could still see with the empty eye socket — newspaper head-lines, bus schedules, anything. He demonstrated this skill at his father's meetings, where the limo driver played the trumpet.

I thought it curious that I had never heard of such a miracle. One would think the word would get around. But perhaps I am always the last to know.

If only I had a story like that. If only I could tell

you about the time I saw God, or the time I heard Him as Abraham or Moses or Paul did. If only I could have my Seeing-Eye-Socket Miracle.

Sadly, all I have is my Shove from Above.

The Shove from Above is not a very good miracle story, but it's all I have. I have not told it to anyone before, but I will tell it to you.

When I was twelve years old, I lived in an Oregon logging town called Butte Falls — population 450. My father was pastor of the Butte Falls Community Church.

That meant I had to go to every Sunday School class, worship service, evening service, potluck, Christmas Eve candlelight service — practically every event on the church calendar.

Having done this for seven years in various churches Dad pastored, I'd collected enough Sunday School attendance pins to reach from my shirt pocket to my belt buckle. I'd heard my father preach so many times I could hear him in my sleep. I'd eaten enough green potluck Jell-O, sung enough verses of "Just As I Am," and cranked enough church bulletins through the mimeograph that I almost deserved to be ordained myself.

One Sunday night, just before evening service, I

couldn't take it anymore. The rest of my family had already disappeared into the church sanctuary, but I hung outside, resisting.

Shoving my hands in my pockets, I dawdled along the darkening fringes of the church property. All was quiet, except for the sound of the church piano.

The sanctuary windows glowed with a warm yellow light, but I was not attracted. Standing at the edge of a ditch that ran along the road, I resolved not to step into that church that night. I would not sing another song from the old maroon hymnbook, listen to another sermon, hear another offertory prayer or testimony or announcement.

Voices rose in unison from the sanctuary. The first hymn was starting, wafting through the open door. I was not moved.

I would take my stand, right here along the ditch. Nothing could make me walk into that service — nothing.

And then it happened.

Suddenly, right between my shoulder blades, I felt a push. Not a gentle tap, but a firm shove. It hit me so hard that I nearly fell into the ditch.

Trying to regain my balance, I leapt across the

ditch onto the church lawn. I looked around to see who had pushed me.

Nobody was there. Nobody I could see, anyway.

My eyes grew wide. But there was no question in my mind what had happened.

God had pushed me. He was telling me to get into that sanctuary, *now.*

My voice was an awed whisper. "OK, OK," I said.

Walking across the dark lawn, I felt more thrilled than chastened. Sure, I'd go to church as I probably should have done in the first place. But the important thing, the huge thing, was that God had just reached down and shoved me. I had felt Him poke me right in the back.

I walked inside and sat in a pew, vibrating, alert. I don't remember what the sermon was about that night, but I know I paid closer attention to it than I had paid to a sermon in years.

I remembered that shove for a long time. I didn't tell anybody about it; I just remembered it. Nothing like that ever happened to me again.

And that is the story of my Shove from Above.

As I said, it's not a very good miracle story.

It's not impressive, like the Seeing-Eye-Socket Miracle. I can't prove that it was really God poking me — that it wasn't a muscle spasm, a gust of wind, or even a figment of my guilty imagination, wanting someone to push me into that church, to make me do the right thing.

It's not demonstrable, like the Seeing-Eye-Socket Miracle. I can't travel with an evangelist and a trumpeter, being pushed across the platform each night by an invisible hand.

It's not even a very good example of God's power at work. Can the God who spoke in such detail to Abraham and Moses communicate with people today only by poking them in the back?

When you get right down to it, it's a pretty lousy miracle story.

But it's *my* story.

Come to think of it, maybe that's important.

After all, that's how I know my account is an honest one. I may not know exactly why I felt shoved that night, but I know I didn't make the story up.

And since it's my story, it has meaning — at least to me. I can't use it to warn others that God will push them for trying to miss a church service, but I've used it more than once to remind myself how important it is to keep meeting with other Christians.

Of course, even though it's my story, it would be a bad one if it contradicted Scripture. But it doesn't seem to. The Bible doesn't say God pushed me, but it doesn't say He didn't or couldn't or wouldn't.

Maybe it's not such a bad story after all.

It's no Seeing-Eye-Socket Miracle. But it's mine. It's part of my history with God, whether He did the shoving or whether He turned my clumsiness into an indelible memory aid.

That's true of your story too.

You know the one I mean.

Maybe it was a story you told the whole church at testimony time, about a growth that had the doctors worried one month, only to shrink and leave them scratching their heads the next.

Maybe it was something you shared in a home Bible study, about the time you woke in the middle of the night, feeling you should pray for your brother, and heard the next day that he had been driving in a snowstorm at that very hour.

Or maybe it was a story you never told anyone, about the night you were swamped with grief, only to feel a sudden presence with you, as if God were putting His arm around you, holding you tight.

Hold onto your story. Like mine, it may seem unimpressive or unprovable to others. But don't let it fade away. Whether or not you tell it to anyone else, tell it to yourself.

If it's honest, if it helps you grow, if it fits with Scripture, treasure it. It has power, your story, more power than a thousand stories someone else might tell. It has power for you because you were there.

Maybe it will bring you peace when it seems God is gone, or that He never knew your name. Maybe it will remind you of the gratitude you owe Him. Maybe it will lead you to complete a good work left undone, undo a wrong, or share His story with someone else.

There's no telling what God might do with our stories, yours and mine, if we only keep remembering and learning from them.

He might even use them to push us in the right direction.

He does that sometimes, you know.

Kodachrome

A MONSTROUS CRIME WAS COMMITTED
against me when I was twelve years old.

Steve Anderson put a dent in the end of my
telescope.

The violation occurred one day at midmorning,
shortly before the Andersons, friends of my parents, were to leave our home after a brief visit. The
telescope was on its tripod in a bedroom, its white
barrel gleaming in the sunlight. It looked like, and
was, my most prized possession.

I had just shown the telescope to the perpetra-
tor-to-be, explaining how I would go to the Butte
Falls High School football field on clear nights and
gaze at the moon's craters and Saturn's rings. Perhaps I mentioned to him that I had become such

an expert in astronomy that my science teacher, Mr. Hawkins, had let me teach the class one day. If so, jealousy must have led the miscreant to the evil act he was about to perform.

Suddenly the younger Anderson siblings entered the room and ran around in circles, no doubt at their older brother's prompting. Using the chaos as an excuse, Steve bumped into the telescope and knocked it to the floor.

The crash of metal against varnished hardwood sent a shock wave straight to my heart. Falling to my knees, I surveyed the damage.

There was the mortal wound: a dent in one side of the black lens hood — not enough to affect viewing, but enough to keep the plastic dust cover from ever fitting precisely again. Moreover, the dust cover itself lay on the floor with a chip broken from its edge!

Enraged, I turned toward Steve. "You owe me sixty dollars!" I screamed, recalling the whole telescope's original purchase price.

The adults pushed into the room. "What's happening here?" my father asked.

Steve looked confused and forlorn — a clever ruse. I reported the facts, then waited for justice.

My father examined the telescope and rendered his verdict. "It was an accident," he said. "And it looks like the telescope will work just fine." As for the sentence, there would be no sixty-dollar fine. There would be no penalty at all.

"But he *broke* it!" I protested.

"It was an *accident*," my mother said, affirming the earlier court's decision. I watched, dumbfounded, as the vandal and his family were allowed to go free.

I vowed not to forget what Steve had done — nor the way my parents had betrayed me. How could they have forgiven when they should have demanded restitution? It was obvious that they didn't understand simple concepts like justice and fairness.

It mattered little that the telescope continued to work. Every time I used it, I saw the dent and remembered.

*   *   *   *

Not long after that, my parents announced that we were going on vacation. It was just what I needed to take my mind off that terrible crime, if only temporarily.

Real vacations had always been too expensive for us, the income of a rural pastor's family being what it was. But this trip was going to be different. This was going to be the vacation we'd all been waiting for, the kind other families took—a trip to California.

Like other families, we planned to capture the event on film. I was an expert in that area, as in astronomy; my best friend Monty, a fellow eighth-grader, had taught me how to develop black-and-white film and prints in a makeshift darkroom off the parsonage porch. But black-and-white pictures would never do for this trip. This was a *color* vacation. We would have to bring back color pictures, just as other families did.

So we bought two rolls of Kodachrome slide film—one for me, one for my parents. After loading our little Instamatic cameras, we headed south on Highway 101.

We stayed in San Jose with the Weavers. Like the Andersons, they were friends of my parents. Unlike the Andersons, they had no delinquent children who had never learned to respect the property of others. It was indeed a real vacation.

That week I took pictures of Lick Observatory

with its two mammoth telescopes — neither of which had a dent. We all took pictures of San Francisco — of the skyscrapers, the famous roller-coaster streets, the Golden Gate Bridge, and the brightly colored fish at the city aquarium.

Then we went home, our Kodachrome packed with once-in-a-lifetime memories. Even if we never took a real vacation again, no one could take away our pictures — not even Steve Anderson.

Before we could send our film off for processing, however, my photo-developing mentor Monty said something that caught my ear.

He'd just bought a kit that allowed anyone with a darkroom to develop color slides. It was easy, he said, almost like black-and-white film. Best of all, I could use his kit in my darkroom — free of charge! The timing was perfect: fast, free processing exactly when we needed it. Being an expert in darkroom technique, as in astronomy, I knew I would have no problem developing my own roll of Kodachrome.

At my request, my parents let me have their roll too. No doubt they knew I would never allow harm to come to the only record of their rare vacation. They knew I — unlike Steve Anderson —

understood the value of others' prized possessions.

After reading the instructions on Monty's kit, I entered the darkroom and closed the door, the first roll of Kodachrome in my hand.

For the next half hour, my performance was indeed expert. I followed each step perfectly, keeping a close watch on the time and on the thermometer in the developing tank. I did everything I was supposed to do.

But when I finished the final step, opened the tank, and gently lifted out the reel that held the film, my breathing stopped.

I stared at that roll of Kodachrome — and stared and stared, even though there was nothing to look at.

There were no pictures on it. Even the numbers on the border had disappeared. I held in my hand a wet strip of clear plastic, the clearest plastic I had ever seen.

Looking in the tank, I saw black sludge settling to the bottom. That was all that was left of this roll of once-in-a-lifetime vacation photographs.

But that was not the worst of it. These were my parents' once-in-a-lifetime vacation photographs.

I had picked up their Kodachrome first.

The finality of it closed on me like the door of a bank vault. I'd destroyed my overworked parents' only record of the one real vacation they'd been able to take in years. I'd ruined something irreplaceable that belonged to someone else.

It was the kind of thoughtless destruction one might expect from . . . Steve Anderson.

With a trembling hand I grabbed the instructions, searching for an explanation. There it was: a paragraph at the bottom of a page, listing the kinds of slide film that could be developed with this kit. There was Ektachrome. There were a few other chromes.

But there was no Kodachrome.

I had used the wrong kit, the wrong chemicals. This kit would have developed a roll of Ektachrome nicely—but not Kodachrome. If I'd read the instructions completely, I would have known that.

This was not the kind of action worthy of an expert. It was the kind of stupid mistake worthy of . . . a kid who thought he knew everything.

I kept staring at that blank roll of film as if trying to will those images back into existence. Maybe

Steve Anderson had felt that way when the telescope hit the floor, wishing he could reverse the law of gravity. But I'd done far more than dent my parents' pictures. I'd wiped them out completely.

I wanted to stay in that darkroom forever. But eventually I had to come out. When I did, my perspective on justice and mercy had been altered somewhat.

I could only hope that my parents' perspective hadn't.

I trudged into the living room. Avoiding my parents' eyes, I tried to explain what had happened. Then I waited, looking at the floor.

There was a disappointed "Oh." And then, softly, "That's OK."

Then came the sentencing: Like Steve Anderson, I was free to go.

I waited for the rest — a lecture about how important those pictures had been, or a warning, or at least a long sigh and a shaking of heads.

It never came.

For months I waited for my parents to bring the incident up again. Surely they would mention it the next time I let them down, the next time I proved that I was not an expert after all.

But they never did.

It was as if the incident had never happened. It was if they had put it as far from them as the east is from the west.

It was as if they'd once made terrible mistakes themselves, and ruined something dear to Someone else, only to have that Someone forgive them and never bring it up again.

It was as if they remembered how it felt to be forgiven, and to have their sins forgotten.

* * * *

More than a quarter of a century has passed since the Kodachrome incident. I'm still waiting for my parents to bring it up, but they never have. I guess they never will.

As for Steve Anderson, I haven't seen him since. I hope he forgave and forgot the way I yelled at him.

And the telescope? After using it for a few more years, I sold it at a garage sale. The person who bought it didn't seem bothered at all by the dent.

The pictures — well, I still have some of the slides I took on that vacation. I sent them *out* to be developed.

But my most important memories of those days

were ones that Kodachrome couldn't capture.
Next time I forget what it feels like to be forgiven,
I'd better pull them out and look them over once
again.

O Holy Nights

WINTER NIGHTS IN THE MOUNTAINS are clear, cold, quiet. That's how they were in Butte Falls, Oregon the year I discovered Christmas.

Most of the 450 residents of our little logging town didn't know it, but their silent nights were about to be disrupted. My father, pastor of the Community Church, had a plan to reach them by playing Christmas carols from the church steeple.

People in our mostly unchurched town probably didn't hear much Christmas music, he guessed — not the right kind, anyway. They didn't even hear it in stores or restaurants, the no-frills Butte Falls General Store and Nora's cafe being the only such establishments in town. There wasn't even any Christmas elevator music; there were no elevators.

It was up to the church to provide Christmas carols. Dad hoped their message could somehow get through.

He got to work, stringing wires from a loudspeaker in the steeple to our family's ancient phonograph in the church entryway. From the parsonage across the street he brought over our collection of worn Christmas records — a stack of just four or five.

Now all he needed was a volunteer — someone to sit in the entryway, manning the phonograph from 7 to 9 P.M. each night during the week before Christmas. It would have to be someone responsible, who wouldn't let the records go on and on until they reached the end and went *scritch, scritch, scritch* for the whole town to hear. It would also have to be someone who didn't mind freezing, because the heat in the church wouldn't be turned on.

There were no volunteers, so I was elected.

I didn't mind too much. Our house was right across the street, so I wouldn't have to go far. I could even think of my assignment as a rite of passage, proof that I had become a man; my brothers Paul and Mark were too young for such a challenge, but I had reached the mature age of twelve.

There were risks, of course — playing a record at the wrong speed, forgetting to put on a new one, bumping the needle and producing a *scrrrrrrippp* that could be heard from one end of town to the other. But the risks just made it more interesting.

The first night Dad and I walked across the icy street to the church. Zipped into a heavy coat, I carried a steel thermos full of hot chocolate Mom had made. Dad showed me how to work the phonograph and got the first record started. Then he left. I was all alone.

I felt like the Wizard of Oz behind his curtain, controlling what a vast and unseen audience would hear. Wondering how the music sounded to that audience, I stepped outside.

Hark, the herald angels sing
Glory to the newborn King!

The sound from the speaker over my head was so loud I thought it might melt the falling snow in midair. But no angry mob of townspeople appeared to protest. Breathing a sigh of relief that fogged the cold air, I stepped back inside.

Soon I'd have to change records. Glancing through the albums I had to choose from, I was intrigued by two.

One was a record of Christmas chimes — a disk of ruby red plastic, not black like the others. I'd never seen a red record before; I hadn't even known one was possible. I'd have to play that one soon.

The other was an album by George Beverly Shea, Billy Graham's crusade soloist — a singer as famous in our house as Frank Sinatra was in others. I liked Mr. Shea's deep voice, even if my parents liked it too. That album was added to my must-play list.

Taking off my gloves to change records, I felt the sting of cold on my fingers. Onto the turntable went the amazing red record.

Chimes rang out, and I went outside to hear them. "The First Noel" was tinny but crisp in the night air, with just a crackle of static. It sounded very Christmasy, I thought; if people had known the record was red, they would have liked it even more.

Later I played the George Beverly Shea album. His warm, low voice poured like honey from the speaker. I listened to the sound level but not the words, concentrating on having the next record ready.

And I always had one ready, even when I wandered up to the dark choir loft where the church bell rope dangled from a hole in the ceiling, tempting me to pull it. I resisted and made it back in time. There was no dead air, no *scritch* of needle echoing in the night. This job was going to be pretty simple after all.

Maybe too simple.

The next night, after no one complained about the music, I was back at the church. But this time it was just a job. The novelty was wearing off; I'd heard all the records at least once. I'd run up and down the choir loft stairs, and I'd even grown jaded to that ruby-red chime album.

Now it was just the music and me, closed up in that cold, dark church.

That was when I began to discover Christmas.

All alone, huddled over the orange glow of the old phonograph's tubes, I could feel the empty church like a cavern around me. It made me feel small, hushed.

I felt like a lighthouse keeper, even the only person alive. All the things that made up

Christmas — warmth and home, wreaths and wish lists, lights and cookies — seemed a world away. Tonight Christmas was a turntable and a handful of records. There was nothing to do but listen.

The amplifier hummed as I put on the George Beverly Shea album. Down came the tone arm, and I listened.

I wonder as I wander down under the sky
How Jesus the Saviour could come for to
die . . .

The voice flowing from the loudspeaker sounded so sad, so alone. The singer's only companion was a lonely oboe that sighed in the distance.

If Jesus had wanted for any wee thing,
A star in the sky or a bird on the wing,
He surely could have it, for He was the King. . . .

Sitting all by myself in the cold, I began to think about the people in our little town who were wondering, wandering, never having met this King.

There was my best friend. There was the town librarian, a tough old lady who guarded her little roomful of books next to the fire station. There were the school dropouts who spent Saturday nights drag-racing up and down the main street; the shop teacher, a Mormon; the loggers, with names like Red, scoffers at religion. There was the town drunk, who sat on the bench outside the only bar, a man whose name nobody seemed to remember.

Were they listening tonight?

I imagined the words floating though the clear, cold air. How far did they go?

For a moment, in my imagination, I floated with the music, looking down at the houses with their smoking chimneys, swooping down to look into the front windows. I saw people drinking eggnog, congratulating themselves on the Christmas trees they had cut in the woods, laughing and being warm and eating homemade fudge and having absolutely no idea what Christmas was all about.

I felt as sad as the singer on the record sounded. Mine was not the sorrow of the searcher, but the sorrow of one who had already found.

How could those people in their living rooms not understand what Christmas was all about? It was all so clear, right there in the carols I was playing. What more could God have done than to send His own Son?

They *had* to hear the music; they *had* to understand. Yet I knew that even if they'd stood directly in front of the loudspeaker, many of them would not have heard — really heard.

Why was that? Why were people bent on wondering and wandering, on hurting themselves and each other in dark little towns like this one when there was so much light to be had?

And just for a moment, sitting on a metal folding chair in front of an old phonograph, sending music into the night, I felt it.

I felt the faintest echo of the way it must have felt to sit in heaven on that night 2,000 years ago, launching the Light into the darkness. I felt a tiny bit of it, the longing for Him to be received, the knowing that He was the only hope, the certainty that so many would cover their eyes and wait for Him to go away.

For an instant I could imagine a love so strong it encompassed a whole world in the dark, so strong it led Him not just to send music but to fly with it, swooping down to peek into our windows and knock on our doors and enter our lives.

In a very small way, and for a very short time, I felt the painful urgency of Christmas. It was Christmas from the Father's side. It was Christmas stripped of everything but a cold night and a warm truth: God so loved the world that He gave His only Son, that whoever believed in Him would not perish but have eternal life.

I had known John 3:16 since I could memorize, but I had never felt Christmas hurt before.

Perhaps it was a rite of passage after all.

When I was a learner, I sought both night and day;
I asked the Lord to aid me, and He showed me the way. . . .

It was the last song on the record. The voice boomed the chorus boldly into the darkness:

Go tell it on the mountain,
Over the hills and everywhere,
Go tell it on the mountain
That Jesus Christ is born.

It became a tradition to play carols from the steeple of the Butte Falls Community Church, to

73

tell it on the mountain with a loudspeaker and a phonograph. No one complained; a few even said they liked it. Most never said what they thought, one way or the other.

For as long as we lived there, every year, I was the one who sat in the cold, dark church and manned the phonograph on the nights before Christmas. It was my job, and I wasn't about to let anybody take it away from me.

Maybe I realized, even then, what a privilege it is to be alone with the truth of Christmas — to think of the Giver as well as the Gift, the pain of rejection as well as the joy of acceptance.

Maybe I realized how hard it is for all of us to let the distractions of Christmas, the wrappings, fall away — to just sit in the dark and listen.

The Hidden Dangers of the Square Dance

WHEN I WAS GROWING UP, the world was a scary place.

Everyone knew the obvious dangers — things like hydrogen bombs, rattlesnakes, and sticking a cotton swab too far into your ear. But only Christians seemed to recognize the truly insidious threats — like dirty jokes, movies, television, swearing, billiards, card-playing, and dancing.

Not that I heard sermons about this list of don'ts, or even lectures from parents or Sunday School teachers. I just *knew* these things were off limits. I *knew* they were the exclusive domain of non-Christians who swilled beer and laughed too loudly in some distant red-light district full of cigarette machines, poker games, billiard parlors, and dance halls.

I knew all this in grade school, without having seen a red-light district, smoked, played poker, stepped into a pool hall, or waltzed. I knew it without having had more than two or three non-Christian friends, none of whom indulged in these activities.

I'm not sure how I knew all this. Perhaps it was the stern warnings in Christian youth magazines, or the way people at church frowned when they mentioned bars and two-piece bathing suits. Whatever my sources, I was greatly certain of a great many things.

And of all these things, I was surest about dancing.

I could see at a glance that true Christians never danced. We were hearers of music — not doers. At the Foothills Community Church we never moved to the beat. Toe tapping and hand clapping were foreign to our sanctuary, even when the Mahan family sang its rousing bluegrass specialty, "Life Is Like a Mountain Railway." We Christians simply did not lose control.

If the idea of dancing in church was appalling, *social* dancing was 10,000 times worse. It was a clear and present danger combining most of the others — lust, alcohol, loud music, smoking, and immodesty. Everyone knew the foul atmosphere of a dance could breed every kind of evil, and usually did.

I knew it even though I had never gotten within half a mile of a sock hop. It was enough to know that dancing was *scary*.

Of that I had proof. I had gotten it one terrible day in fifth grade.

That was the day our physical education teacher made a shocking announcement. We would be doing something a little different for the next several weeks, he said.

We would be learning to dance.

Boys and girls together.

Starting that very day.

There had been no warning, no time to run. I was trapped — and as threatened as if Soviet troops had burst through the doors and declared that all students would embrace atheism or be shot on the spot.

I could not protest. When I opened my mouth, no sound came out.

I was outnumbered. Everyone else was *them,*

and I was the only *us*.

They were worldly, cool, comfortable. *I* was the backward, inexperienced preacher's kid.

They would know exactly what to do when the dancing started. *I* would be lost, humiliated.

As generic music began to crackle from a phonograph in the corner of the gym, I felt myself hurtling into unknown territory. Numbly I followed as boys and girls formed separate circles facing each other. The circles reeled this way, then that. Somehow we were paired off.

The teacher's instructions were barely audible over the music. *Walk right, walk left. Walk with your partner in a line. Change partners. No, not that way. Turn around.*

By the time class was done that day, I was exhausted, confused. But I knew one thing: Dancing was dangerous. Evil. And most of all, scary.

And no one would force me to do it again. Ever.

When I told my parents what had happened, their reaction was calm. If I wanted to stay away from the class because of my personal beliefs, they said, they would write me an excuse. But it was up to me.

Of *course* I wanted an excuse, I said. I *had* to have one. It was nice that they wanted me to make up

my own mind about these things, but I was in
danger!

Armed with my excuse, I spent the next several
weeks of P.E. time in the library — reading books,
doing homework, and feeling safe.

It was comforting to know that I would never be
trapped in such a scary spot again. The rules would
protect me. Rules of right and wrong. Rules that
separated *us* from *them*. Rules that had to be
obeyed.

And the rules might have saved me, if not for an
even more terrible day three years later.

Our eighth-grade class was coming back from an
all-day field trip. It was late afternoon, still an hour
or so from our little town of Butte Falls, Oregon.
Several of us were wedged into our teacher's car,
watching the scenery go by.

Suddenly someone noticed a hand-painted sign
on a building down the road.

SQUARE DANCING, it said.

It was clear from the cars parked outside the
building that the dance was underway. For my
classmates it was the perfect opportunity to make
the field trip last a little longer.

"Hey," said one. "Let's go square dancing!"

"Yeah!" said another.

My mouth went dry.

There was a chorus of agreement. Soon all in the car had spoken on the subject — except the teacher and me.

"Well," the teacher said, "we *could* go for a while and not get back too late."

There was a pause, as if everyone were waiting for me to say something. I swallowed. The car seemed hotter and more cramped with each second.

"Uh," I mumbled, "I don't think. . . . "

The teacher looked back over the front seat and raised his eyebrows. "Oh, come on," he said, trying to sound casual. *"Square* dancing isn't against your religion, is it?"

I squirmed in the seat as my brain went into overdrive. Ransacking my memory for a rule, I found none.

I didn't even know what square dancing was.

Was it something farmers and pioneers did, like quilting? If so, maybe it wasn't exactly *social* dancing. . . .

But that wasn't the important thing. What mattered was that I didn't know anything about it. I'd never done it. I didn't know how to do it.

If we stopped at the SQUARE DANCING sign, it would be like that day in the fifth grade. I would be the one who didn't fit, the one who didn't know what to do. I would risk being laughed at, shamed.

I needed a rule to protect me, to keep me safe. But I wasn't sure there was one.

So I pretended to be sure.

Yes, I told the teacher. Square dancing *was* against my religion.

Then I turned to the window, my face burning.

Disappointed sighs filled the car. The teacher turned back to watch the road, shrugged, and said OK.

For the rest of the trip, nobody mentioned square dancing. But I could think of nothing else.

Staring at the fir trees that flashed by, I felt more shamed than if we had stopped.

I had no idea how Jesus felt about square dancing. But I knew how He felt about lying.

I was safe, all right.

And sorry.

* * * *

Sometimes it hurts to see the Light.

Sometimes a bright shaft catches you, pierces you, and will not let you go.

Even when you prefer the darkness.

That's what happened to me that day in the car, when the light exposed a lie. Only I could see it, and I see it to this day.

I still wonder what happened to that teacher, to those students, because of my *yes*.

Did they take me at my word, and avoid this strange "religion" that condemned the most old-fashioned pastimes? Did they decide the church had nothing to offer but rules? Did the dividing line I'd drawn help keep them away from God for good?

Things might have been so different if I'd found the strength to say three words I find so hard to say: *I don't know*.

I wonder what would have happened.

I wonder what would happen today if all the Christians like me were a little less afraid, a little less certain, a little less eager to make up rules and sign the name of Jesus to them.

The world would still be a scary place.

But maybe, just maybe, a few more people might want to be *us* instead of *them*.

A few more people might be safe.

Not just now, but for eternity.

Pastor Ted

THINGS WERE GOING SO WELL for Ted Zabel in 1968.

It was a shame that I had to mess them up.

For several record-setting years Ted had served as youth director at Salem Alliance Church in Salem, Oregon. With his energized, energizing personality and steady reliance on God he'd built a large and spiritually growing youth group. No wonder he strode around with a big smile on his face, bursting with optimism and ideas, telling everybody the latest elephant jokes he'd heard from the junior highers.

But then I came to town.

I was sixteen. And I was angry—angry at everything Ted Zabel stood for.

I hadn't always been that way. Until recently I'd been a model youth group member; I was a preacher's kid, after all. But that had changed a few months ago. Everything had changed.

After eleven years of planting and nurturing churches in little logging towns and farming areas, my father had learned that he faced a possible heart attack. He had to get some rest, the doctor said. Dad knew there was no point in asking his mission board for sick leave; they'd turned him down once before, telling him they didn't believe in that sort of thing.

He'd had no choice but to resign. His career as a pastor was over — just like that. We'd moved to Salem without jobs or income, and seemingly without a future.

My anger at the mission board knew no bounds. It spilled over, coloring the way I saw the world, especially the church. When my parents chose Salem Alliance as our new church home, it was inevitable: Ted Zabel and I were on a collision course.

Despite my bitterness, I couldn't imagine skipping church entirely — even if my parents had been willing to let me. Going to church was part of me, like wearing shoes instead of going barefoot. I started showing up at youth group functions, hanging back at the edge of things, reluctant to take part.

That was where I met Pastor Ted. Everybody called him that — not Pastor Zabel, and certainly not Reverend. Those titles never would have fit a man whose idea of fun was to take a home movie of kids eating hot dogs and run it in reverse, so that the kids appeared to be regurgitating. Official-sounding terms like *clergy* and *man of the cloth* didn't seem to apply to him as he sat at the movie projector, his tall frame folded onto a chair, running the hot dog film backward and listening to the guys laugh and the girls go *Eeeeewwwww.* Only a Pastor Ted would do that, grinning a grin that showed every inch of his teeth and wrinkling his nose as if to say, "Isn't that the most disgusting thing you ever saw, and wouldn't you like to see it again?"

Watching, I knew I could never tell anyone in this group about the deep waters my family and I were wading through. I could never tell them how I felt. No one would understand — not the fun-and-games kids, and certainly not the overgrown kid who led them.

My impression didn't change when, before long, Ted came to our house to call. It was one of those welcome-to-the-group calls, the kind I knew pastors had to make. *It's just his job,* I thought. He had a list of kids to visit, and my next turn would come in a year or so.

But soon Ted was back, knocking at our screen door, flashing that mischievous grin. Again there was small talk about how he was looking forward to getting to know us. I didn't buy it, but sensed he'd gone out of his way to see us again. What was he up to?

Next he did the unthinkable. He asked me to do him a favor — to write funny announcements in the youth group's weekly newsletter.

How could he ask such a thing? Didn't he know how angry I was? Hadn't he seen my sullen face at every youth group event? Somehow Ted had overlooked that. In doing so, he'd hit on the one assignment that could have attracted me. I said yes, dreaming of how I might poke fun at the church and its program from the safety of my new position.

I started churning out announcements that needled the other kids and Ted himself. Instead of pulling the plug, Ted became my cheerleader. Again he visited our house, claiming that people throughout the church looked forward to reading my hilarious news roundups every Sunday.

I found that hard to believe. But I knew he wasn't paid to make compliments like that. Why was he doing this? What was he after?

Then there was another assignment, and another. Hearing that I liked to draw, Ted asked whether I'd make posters to publicize youth group events. It was a job he'd reserved for himself, having studied art in college. I took it, and wondered why he was giving it up.

He asked me to play the guitar with a musical group he was forming, and I agreed. My strumming was barely audible, my chord changes clumsy, but he let me play on. Again I wondered: With plenty of skilled musicians in the church, why had Ted chosen me?

Before I knew it, I was one of the busiest kids in the youth group. I was on this committee, in that skit, leading that discussion. I still frowned most of the time, but I was involved. Eventually the other kids, perhaps mistaking my seriousness for spirituality, elected me president of the group.

It was crazy. Didn't these people know how I felt about the church? Didn't they realize that my family was still wandering in a wilderness of unemployment and uncertainty?

Of course they didn't know. Two years after my father had been forced to leave the ministry, I still couldn't talk about it.

The end of my senior year was approaching. Ted came to me with a final project: a Youth Booth, a rented space at the state fair meant to attract teenagers to the Good News. Ted wanted to know: Would I put together a slide show to get people to the booth? Would I come up with a sound track for the slides, make a sign for the booth, and write a low-key, funny tract to be given out?

Once again he had chosen just the right assignment. I took it on and wondered one more time: Why was he giving so much responsibility to me? What *was* Ted Zabel trying to accomplish, anyway?

For weeks I sorted through boxes of slides, chose songs, and clicked the slide projector's remote control until every muscle in my hand ached. I wrote the tract and spent hours drawing the big YOUTH BOOTH sign with a little fine-line pen and a small brush.

As the opening day of the fair drew near, there was only one thing left to do: paint the sheet of plywood onto which the slides would be projected.

On a Saturday afternoon I went to the church. I got down on my hands and knees in an empty hallway, using a roller to spread white paint on that vast expanse of plywood. The only sound was the wet *skish, skish* of the roller. Then I heard another sound — a key in a door, some footsteps. And there was Pastor Ted, standing next to me.

We talked about the project, as we had talked about so many projects in the past two years. Suddenly I saw how much we had been through together, Pastor Ted and I.

He'd always been there, putting up with my mocking and mumbling, feeling the effects of my anger but never responding in kind. He'd spent time with me that he didn't have to spend, even with dozens of other kids to worry about and hundreds of other things to do.

He'd ignored the way I was and focused on what I might become.

And all at once I was ready, ready to talk about what had happened to my father, to my family, to me.

89

So I talked, and Ted listened.

I kept painting as I talked, determined not to break down as I let the anger out, and the roller went *skish, skish, skish* long after I finished. For a while it was the only sound in the whole church.

I don't remember what Ted said when he finally spoke. I only remember that I could hear the sadness in his voice. He didn't have to say he understood; when I looked up I could see it in his face. The ever-present smile was gone, replaced by a reflection of the pain I'd held inside.

At last someone had stopped and listened and understood. Like so many people, that was all I'd wanted.

Ted had gotten close enough to let it happen. He had done it with a lot of projects and a lot more patience.

Now I knew what he'd been up to.

*　*　*　*

Years later I worked as an intern next to Ted and the rest of the Salem Alliance staff. At one staff meeting the need for people to do projects was discussed. When talk began to focus on recruiting volunteers, Ted had a quiet comment.

"I don't believe in getting things done through people," he said. "I believe in getting people done through things."

He didn't point me out as an example. But he could have.

Thanks, Pastor Ted.

Things Change

I'D ALWAYS WANTED TO BE A WRITER.

Well, not always. First I'd wanted to be a cowboy, then a pastor, then a magician, then a scientist. But that was before I hit junior high. From then on, thanks to Mark Twain and C.S. Lewis, Edgar Rice Burroughs, and Joseph Bayly, I wanted to write.

No one affirmed this path by giving me a Big Chief writing tablet like John-Boy got on "The Waltons," but I had plenty of encouragers along the way. My parents. English teachers. Even a vice principal who pulled me out of class and sat me down with a Dylan Thomas story he loved — just so I'd see the possibilities, the power, of words.

I believed in that power, and longed to use it to send the most important messages in the world.

The truths of the Bible. The Good News about Jesus. Ideas most people didn't seem to pay attention to, because they thought they'd heard them all before.

Maybe I could say some of those things in new ways, I thought. Surprising ways that would get people's attention. I was too quiet to make much of an impression by talking, but maybe I could reach people by writing.

With that dream in mind, I decided to study journalism and English. Off I went to a small liberal arts school not far from my hometown.

There I began to learn about grammar, syntax, composition, and poetry. I signed up for classes in interviewing, reporting, editing, photojournalism, broadcasting, and a host of other subjects.

But I would also take a course that didn't appear in the college catalog. It would teach me something the other classes couldn't. Something about plans and dreams like mine. And all goals that aim to somehow honor God.

The course began one morning two months into the semester, when I found a message in my campus mailbox. It was typed on a slip of paper:

Please come to the president's office at 2 this afternoon. He would like to meet with you.

Nervousness knotted my stomach as I read and reread the note. What could the president of the college want with me? I'd done nothing to distinguish myself so far — no records set, no rules broken. I knew the president was a busy and brilliant man — a Rhodes scholar, according to the college catalog. He couldn't possibly want to see me.

But there was the summons, with my name on it. The knot in my stomach tightened as I slipped the message into my pocket.

Glancing at the rest of the mail, I saw nothing important — just a bulletin from my home church, with a Sunday School paper called *Power for Living* stapled inside. Sliding the paper into a notebook, I headed for my next class.

Shortly before 2 that afternoon I sat in the waiting area outside the president's office. My palms were icy, my mouth dry.

"The president will see you now," the secretary said at last.

Still carrying my notebook, I rose and ventured into the inner office.

The president was sitting behind his desk, a big desk. He looked as he had during his speech to the student body at the beginning of the school

95

year—dignified, controlled, even aristocratic.

He invited me to sit. I went to a nearby sofa, but he redirected me to the chair in front of his desk. Squeaking something apologetic, I sat down. An awkward silence followed.

Finally he spoke. "You're interested in communications," he said evenly.

I stammered something about being good at written communication, not verbal.

His smile was condescending. "Oral," he said.

"Pardon me?"

"Oral communication. *Verbal* can refer to either written or spoken communication."

"Oh," I said faintly. My confidence, already ebbing, hit bottom.

With brisk efficiency he moved to the subject of the meeting: reassuring me, as a journalism student, that rumored cutbacks in that department had not been finalized yet. There would still be good reasons to continue my studies here, he said, even if the cutbacks were made. He was telling me this because my high school counselor, an alumnus, had heard the rumors and expressed concern.

I felt relieved. So that was it. Just the journalism program. Nothing personal.

My relief had come too soon.

"Tell me," he said, looking distracted. "What do you intend to do after you graduate?"

I froze. I knew what my goal was, but not how to put it. *I want to be a writer* sounded too simple-minded. So did *I want to be a Christian writer*.

Looking down at the notebook in my lap, I suddenly remembered the Sunday School paper I'd stuck there — the copy of *Power for Living* that had come in the mail. I pulled it out and held it up.

"I want to write material like this," I said. Scanning the cover, I noticed that the lead article didn't look too interesting that week. "Only better," I added.

The president looked at the paper I was holding up. Then he looked at me. Finally he looked away, toward the ceiling, and the condescending smile on his lips grew more pronounced.

"Well," he said, as if speaking to a child who simply didn't know better, "we all change our goals."

It took a few moments for his words to sink in. But when they did, I felt as if he'd laughed aloud at me.

It was as if he'd called his fellow educators over and said, *Look at this one! He wants to write religious propaganda. Imagine wasting a college*

97

education on such a mindless career. But give
him time. He'll grow up, and leave it all behind.

Slowly I put the little Sunday School paper back
in my notebook. I stared at the carpet. So this was
what sophisticated people, really smart people,
thought of my goal. I'd received my report card, di-
rect from the president: My dreams deserved a failing grade.

I don't remember what else was said that afternoon. The meeting was more or less over.

All I recall is the feeling that something in me
marked *Fragile* had been thrown against the wall. I
didn't know yet whether it had broken.

*   *   *   *

The president was right, of course. Things do
change. Goals. Plans. People.

Things changed drastically for the president
himself. Shortly after I graduated from that college, he lost his job. A no-confidence vote from the
faculty nudged him from office.

I hope he weathered that change, and found ful-
fillment in a new career. I can't help but think that
he had to change his goals — at least some of them.

As for the fumbling freshman who stammered

his way through that meeting in the president's office nearly twenty-five years ago, he is sitting in front of a computer, writing this story.

He went through some changes too. After graduation he tried a series of jobs, most of them unrewarding. Eventually he moved 2,000 miles away from his hometown and his college. He wound up as the editor of a little Sunday School paper. The kind churches sometimes staple into bulletins and put in the mail. A paper called *Power for Living*.

These days, though, he writes. He writes a lot of things. He especially likes writing a column for a publication he used to edit. A little Sunday School paper called *Power for Living*. He hopes his columns are like the article he held up in the president's office. Only a tiny bit better.

Things change. And you just never know how they might turn out.

That's why you and I need to hang on to our goals, our dreams. Especially the ones that seek to honor God. Others may laugh, or frown, or give us looks of condescension. But if God is in our goals, all the naysayers in the world can't keep the barricades propped up. Unless we let them.

Long ago another educator, a man so smart he

could have been a Rhodes scholar, had the right idea. His name was Gamaliel, and he was a Pharisee. When his fellow teachers wanted to bury a little band of dreamers who called themselves apostles, this is what he said:

"Therefore, in the present case I advise you: Leave these men alone! Let them go! For if their purpose or activity is of human origin, it will fail. But if it is from God, you will not be able to stop these men; you will only find yourselves fighting against God" (Acts 5:38-39).

Not all our goals are the same as God's. Sometimes ours need to change — radically.

But never just because someone snickered, or groaned, or shook his head.

Next time others try to stick a needle in your dreams, relax. They, not you, may be in for the rude awakening.

As Job once told the Lord,

"I know that You can do all things; no plan of Yours can be thwarted" (Job 42:2).

That's one thing that never changes.

The Third Rose

THE POTENT SMELLS OF FULL-BLOOMED
orchids and carnations hung heavy in the air as I
stepped into the florist's shop. Frowning at the price
cards taped to the glass cases, I saw roses were more
of a luxury than I'd expected — a major outlay for a
college senior with an anemic bank account.

Especially one who expected no return on the
investment he was about to make.

Finally I turned to the man behind the counter.
"I'll take two roses," I said. "And could you deliver
them to the campus on Valentine's Day?"

He promised to do his best — though February
14 was just forty-eight hours away, and *so* many
students were sending flowers to their
sweethearts.

I wrote down the dorm and room number, scribbled *Happy Valentine's Day* on a card, handed over the money, and left. I didn't feel like telling the florist that these two roses were different from all the others he would deliver. They weren't going to a sweetheart.

I didn't have a sweetheart.

All I had was Liz.

I wasn't sure what to call Liz, but *sweetheart* didn't apply. Neither did *girlfriend.* After all this time, none of the romantic terms fit. I wouldn't let them.

After all, Liz Morton wasn't a Christian.

She was a wonderful girl, but she didn't know Jesus. In the year since we'd met, I'd never been able to tell her about Him.

And time was running out.

*   *   *   *

When I'd discovered Liz the year before, as we'd acted in a school play, I didn't think there would be problems. All I knew was that this freshman theater major fascinated me.

Any guy would have been intrigued, I thought. Even surrounded by other student actresses, she

102

had a uniquely natural glamour — long, honey-blond hair, blinding smile, wide green eyes that could switch from sultry to mischievous at a whim. She was petite, just the right shape, a compact bundle of outgoing energy.

She also had an easy-to-please sense of humor. I knew that because she laughed at my jokes, even the lamest ones, when we found ourselves at the local greasy spoon with other cast members after rehearsals. On the list of qualities I found endearing, laughing at my jokes ranked near the top.

But I could tell from stray comments she and others made that she lacked one crucial trait. She wasn't a Christian.

I knew that meant we couldn't get serious. If there was anything I'd learned from sitting through all those church youth group talks on dating, it was the 2 Corinthians 6:14 warning against being unequally yoked with unbelievers.

I also knew Liz would *stay* an unbeliever, if her spiritual state depended on me. I was no evangelist, as my fumbling attempts to witness to classmates in the past had proven. I wasn't about to try converting this sophisticated young woman who was obviously happy with the way her life was going. She wouldn't be interested.

But that didn't mean I couldn't ask her out, did it?

We'd just have fun. Nothing serious. No deep feelings, no wrestling over faith — just casual friendship. Goodnight kisses would be *verboten* — and so would the Four Spiritual Laws.

I'd still be free to keep searching for that special someone I'd dreamed about and prayed for since I was a kid. That Christian girl, somewhere out there, handpicked for me by God — or so I hoped. Someday I would meet her, and she would share my deepest feelings, my longings, my beliefs.

I didn't know who she might be. I only knew she wouldn't be Liz Morton.

So I asked Liz out. She accepted — once, twice, repeatedly. On our dates I made sure things stayed strictly on the surface. We playacted constantly, pretending we were other people, talking with foreign accents, mimicking movie stars.

It was great fun. Through it all, the door to my feelings and my faith stayed bolted shut as planned. I would not fall for her, I told myself. Not even if she was the sweetest, loveliest, most charming girl I'd ever met.

When the school year ended, I breathed a sigh of relief. Liz was thinking about transferring to another college; I probably wouldn't see her again. It was time to get on with my hunt for the *right* girl.

But that fall, Liz was back.

I was surprised, but unconcerned. *No problem,* I thought. *If we went out again, nothing would change.*

And it didn't. Our dates were as silly and meaningless as ever. We played characters, pretended to be space aliens, and on Halloween roamed the campus dressed as Groucho Marx and Mae West.

But as autumn headed toward winter, I began to feel time slipping away. I was a senior now. If I was going to find that girl of my dreams, that Christian who would spend the rest of her life with me, I'd have to start searching in earnest.

I'd have to date a Christian.

Girls like that didn't seem easy to find on our campus. I found one, though — a smart, pretty freshman. She was comfortable to be around, and fun. Soon I was seeing her once a week — and Liz once a week too.

It was heady stuff, dating two girls. But after a few months I wasn't the only one seeing other people. Liz was starting to go out with a guy named Glen. I knew because I'd spotted them at the movies — when I was there with the Christian girl.

Fine, I told myself. *Maybe they belong together. They have so much in common — being non-Christians and all.*

As for me, I'd stick with the present arrangement — as long as it seemed to be working.

But as I entered the home stretch — my final semester — I realized it wasn't working at all. Instead of having two relationships, I had none.

The Christian girl was thoughtful and attractive, but no real romance seemed to be growing between us. It was almost as if something, or someone, was standing in the way.

And Liz — well, Liz had always been out of the question. Besides, there was Glen now. I could never compete with him — not that I wanted to, of course.

So this is how it will end, I thought. In a few months I would graduate, and it would all be over. I'd be left only with the memories of dates that had led nowhere. I'd leave college as I'd entered it: alone, wondering whether God really did have anyone out there for me after all.

Now, walking home from the florist's shop, I had to wonder why I'd ordered those flowers for Liz. We had a history, all right, but no future.

If there was a reason for those two roses, I didn't know what it was.

Yet.

*   *   *   *

Valentine's Day was a working one for me, spent dogging the steps of a reporter at a nearby newspaper where I was interning. That evening I dragged myself back to campus, wondering whether the florist's delivery truck had made it.

Should I go to Liz's room and check? No, it would look as if I were fishing for thanks. But maybe it wouldn't hurt if I just walked past her dorm, in the unlikely event that she was wandering out front.

Curiously, I found her doing just that. Seeing me approach in the deepening twilight, she looked beautiful as ever — but flustered.

"Uh, hi," she said.

I waited, but she didn't mention any roses. Thinking the florist had let me down, I asked, "Didn't you get the flowers?"

107

"Yes," she said, sounding grateful but nervous. There was another awkward pause.

I frowned. *What was going on here? Was she waiting for someone else?*

For Glen, maybe?

Abruptly she asked, "How about coming in and having some popcorn and hot chocolate?"

My frown deepened. *Maybe she is waiting for Glen,* I thought, *but doesn't want me to be here when he shows up.* Even as I followed her inside, a weary sadness was growing somewhere in my chest. Somewhere near my heart.

In her room I sat on one of the beds. I glanced at the dresser. Sure enough, there was a vase. Holding the roses. Red roses.

All three of them.

Blinking, I looked again.

There were three roses. Not two.

Suddenly I felt anger, anger that surprised me. *I ordered two roses, not three,* I thought. Were these from Glen? Had the delivery truck brought his, but not mine? Or were two of them from me, and one from Glen?

Looking worried, Liz emptied the contents of the popcorn popper into a couple of bowls. I sat in silence, my jaw clenched. The heaviness around my heart expanded until it seemed to fill the whole room.

"What's the matter?" Liz kept asking, her wide eyes clouding. I couldn't seem to tell her. I was trying to figure it out myself.

It didn't make sense. I couldn't be jealous. Liz was a non-Christian. Just for fun. No deep feelings, no wrestling over faith. No future.

Before I could speak, there was a knock at the door. It was a girl from across the hall.

"Look at those roses!" she cried. "John, did you give those to Liz? Or did Glen give them to her?"

I winced. *So it wasn't just me,* I thought. *Anyone could see what was going on.*

"Oh, *I* know," the girl said to Liz. "I bet Glen gave you some and John gave you some and you put them all in the same vase. Very convenient!" With a laugh and a wave she left, closing the door behind her.

The silence and sadness in the room were deafening.

Gazing at that third rose and hearing the echoes of an offhand joke, I began to see just where I stood. I was on a cliff, on the verge of losing Liz, on the edge of never seeing her again and knowing that she would spend her life with someone else, not me.

And for the first time, I admitted that I could not bear the thought.

How could I never again see the face that had become such a longed-for sight, never bask in the warmth of that solar smile, never hear that wind-chime laughter over some silly acting game we were turning into an adventure? How could I never once embrace her, never hold her close and tell her how I really felt?

But it would never work. I'd always known that.

And now it was too late. Even as the bunker that had kept her out and kept me in was starting to crumble, it was too late. I'd waited too long to say what needed to be said, to tell the truth about the One I claimed to follow, and now someone else was taking her away from me.

My whole body ached. I felt empty. There was nothing left to do except leave.

"I have to be going," I said, and slowly got to my feet.

"Please tell me what's bothering you," she pleaded. "Don't go." There was a long pause, as if she were hesitating to open a door, unsure of what might lie beyond it.

And then she broke the rule, the rule she'd never heard from me but must have sensed.

"I really care about you," she whispered.

I looked at her, at that precious face, into those honest eyes. The last stones around my heart gave way, and as they did, the feelings and the faith at last were free.

"I . . . think we need to talk," I said.

We did talk that night, just the two of us, sitting on a tattered red couch in the lounge of her dorm. We talked for hours, without tiring, of a Savior who knew all about love, and who had given everything for it. I listened to myself say the words I had feared saying for so long, and marveled that they came so easily.

One week later, after learning all she could about this Savior from a borrowed New Testament, Lizabeth Jane Morton closed her wide, green eyes and placed all her trust in Him.

She prayed a simple prayer, sitting on an old, overstuffed rocking chair in the middle of my dorm room. When she was done, we lifted our heads.

And I found myself bursting into tears.

111

"I think . . . I'm falling in love with you," I said, and then couldn't say any more.

She didn't understand why I was crying. But there would be plenty of time to explain. Time to explain that God had given me a last-minute chance, a chance I didn't deserve.

A chance to find that Christian girl I'd dreamed of, prayed for, all those years.

*   *   *   *

It was just a mixup, that third rose.

Glen hadn't sent it. The florist had — by mistake.

I can't help thinking, though, that Someone made sure things happened that way. Someone who knew it would take a rose to break down a wall and let in the Light.

Liz and I have been married nearly twenty years now. On many of those twenty Valentine's Days I've given her roses — real ones, silk ones, gold ones, even chocolate ones.

If she's tired of roses, she's been too sweet to complain.

Or maybe they remind her too how one night long ago, God showed us both how much He cared — by giving us the Valentine gift of a lifetime.

112

Message from the Mountain

IT WAS THE BIGGEST NEWS STORY of the year, and we were part of it.

At least we *felt* like part of it. The eyes of the world were focused on Mount St. Helens, just ninety miles northeast of us. *Our* volcano was starting to awaken, trembling and venting steam. Suddenly *our* mountain was famous, and in a way we felt a little famous too.

True, the mountain itself was in southwestern Washington State, and we lived in Oregon. But that was close enough. From our vantage point in Salem, Liz and I could feel like part of the action — at a safe distance.

We found it easy to keep in touch with the excitement. Liz's job as a radio news reporter gave her quick access to updates on the mountain's latest wheezes and tremors. At least once a day she called the National Park Service spokesman and aired his comments, and down the hall from her little newsroom an Associated Press teletype chittered out stories about the mountain-related people and places that were fast becoming household names.

We were fascinated with the parade of instant celebrities. There was Harry Truman, a gruff and profane eighty-four-year-old who lived at the foot of the volcano and swore he'd never leave. There were scientists who appeared nightly on Portland TV with their maps and charts and their definitions of exotic terms like *pyroclastic flow.* There were self-proclaimed psychics who predicted and repredicted whether and when St. Helens would erupt. There were hucksters selling T-shirts and other souvenirs to the crowds who clamored to get as close as they could to the smoking, quaking phenomenon.

Soon it was a carnival, a great circus with the mountain as the main attraction. Liz and I were glad to have a front-row seat, rehashing daily the latest developments she'd discovered from phone visits with officials and by "ripping the wire" — tearing stories from the AP teletype for possible use on the air.

As the weeks wore on, voices of discontent were heard on the carnival midway. Sightseers grumbled over the establishment of the Red Zone, an area twenty miles in diameter with the volcano at its center. Access was limited to a few scientists and photographers who were officially taking the mountain's pulse — along with the stubborn Harry Truman.

The suspense was hard to take. *Will we get to see a major eruption?* we wondered. Or would these minor quakes, these little puffs of ash and steam continue forever? Would the mountain ever act like a *real* volcano?

On May 18, 1980, our answer came — with a vengeance.

At 8:32 on that Sunday morning, Mount St. Helens exploded with the force of 500 Hiroshima bombs. Hot gases, ash, and rock shot out of the mountain's side and top at speeds of up to 200 miles per hour, flattening forests for 200 square miles, burying everything beneath a gray, 1,200-degree ash blanket up to 200 feet deep.

The column of ash rose as high as 60,000 feet, but low clouds kept us from seeing it that day. The explosion was audible as far away as 200 miles, but for some reason we didn't hear it.

Within a couple of hours, though, we knew what had happened. TV pictures were unavailable at first, so we glued ourselves to the radio and followed the unfolding drama.

If things had seemed exciting before, they were like a thrill ride now. We were close enough to be part of history, but far enough away to feel unthreatened.

Early reports said a number of people were missing and had probably lost their lives. That was too bad, of course — but we didn't know those people. This was not a time to mourn; it was a time to get caught up in the excitement of a once-in-a-lifetime event.

The massive column of ash blew eastward, missing us. We watched on TV as "Black Sunday" hit Yakima, Washington with a thick cloud of ash that cut visibility to zero and put countless vehicles out of commission.

But not ours. We checked our car's air filter frequently, but hadn't received enough ash to do any harm.

It was all over the national news that night — our mountain, our volcano, our moment in history. Damage estimates were reaching a billion dollars.

As many as sixty people were missing. President Carter would soon fly in to view the devastation.

We weren't devastated, though — just fascinated. It was like a disaster movie, the best one we'd ever seen.

Next morning, Monday, Liz went to work. There was plenty of news to report. Article after article cranked from the teletype. Liz tore them from the machine, sorting them for possible broadcast.

One of those times, ripping the wire copy, she saw the story that stopped our thrill ride cold.

A man named Reid Blackburn was missing on the mountain, the story said. He was a newspaper photographer on loan to the U.S. Geological Survey and *National Geographic* magazine. He'd been taking pictures of the volcano, and now no one knew where he was.

Liz stared in disbelief at the ragged sheet of newsprint in her hand. Reid was a friend of ours from college. We hadn't known he was on the mountain. Last time we'd heard from him, the year before, he had been about to get married.

When Liz called me with the news, the bottom seemed to drop out of my stomach. *This wasn't possible,* I thought. *Not Reid. Not the guy who'd*

117

taken so many perfect pictures for the college newspaper when I'd been the editor. Not the guy with the reddish-brown beard and the wilderness hiker's wardrobe and the sardonic sense of humor.

Reid had chronicled our college years in photographs, brilliant black-and-white images that left no doubt he would have a long and distinguished career as a photojournalist. Liz and I still had quite a few of those pictures — performances in plays, the two of us smiling in the school newspaper office, even one with Reid and others posing for the yearbook as a mythical family of which I was supposedly the patriarch.

We would see Reid again, we told ourselves. We had to. He was just missing, that was all. He would be found, and we could all go back to seeing the volcano as a wild and wonderful adventure.

For the next two days Liz watched the teletype, afraid of what she might see, hoping for good news. Finally, on Thursday, the awaited story appeared, letter by letter, line by line.

Reid was gone. They had found his body eight miles from the crater. He had snapped four pictures, made it to his car, and died in the wave of superheated gases and ash. His car was entombed, up to the windows, in a sea of sandy gray.

Liz felt numb as she read the brief report. Later, in the radio station's bathroom, she cried hard but silently. She thought especially of the wife Reid had left behind, married for just nine months.

I wept too when I heard the news. I felt hollow, helpless, mortal.

And guilty.

Until we'd known that Reid was missing, all the casualties had been only numbers to us. All the homes destroyed, the lives disrupted, had seemed like a TV miniseries, complete with state-of-the-art special effects, and we had been among its most faithful fans.

All of that was history as we went to Reid's memorial service the following week in Vancouver, Washington. An eerie silence seemed to hang over the city; many pedestrians were still wearing dust masks to keep the ash out of their lungs. The service was the saddest I had ever seen, with family and friends and fellow employees from the Vancouver *Columbian* grieving the loss of the young man whose masterful photographs were displayed in the church entryway.

In the weeks that followed, however, most of the world seemed not to notice the loss. Life went on, with many still seeing the disaster as a piece of entertainment, just as we had. Entrepreneurs scooped up the volcanic ash, selling it in vials and melting it into glass paperweights. Others sold cartooned T-shirts saying I SURVIVED MT. ST. HELENS, MAY 18, 1980. Still others wrote tongue-in-cheek songs about the mountain and about Harry Truman, who went from folk hero to legend, buried far beneath the endless gray.

The volcano continued to tremble with minor eruptions; one left a thin layer of ash on our lawn, our car, our house. For a few clear days we could even walk to the end of our block, look north, and see the pillar of white-gray ash rising from the mountain into the deep-blue sky. It looked almost beautiful.

Almost.

In time Mount St. Helens became old news, except for stories about how the vegetation and wildlife seemed to be returning to the mountain's moonlike surface. But Reid did not return, and we found little to celebrate.

Years later I flew over the mountain on my way to Portland. The now-dormant volcano was snow-covered, capped with clouds. It looked squat and rounded, ordinary.

"For those of you on the right side of the aircraft, that's Mount St. Helens," the pilot said over the loudspeaker. Few people craned their necks to get a glimpse. Most were looking at Mt. Hood, on the other side of the plane, which looked so much prettier.

But I gazed at the sleeping volcano, and remembered.

*   *   *   *

It's so easy to forget.

It's so easy to forget that life on earth is not a carnival, not a cabaret. It's easy to imagine that it will last forever — even when we've read enough of the Bible to know it won't.

It's easy to treat the planet's headlong rush toward the end as a sideshow — the last wonder of the world, a fireworks display to beat them all, something to watch from a safe distance and be glad we aren't part of.

It's easy to spend too much time strolling through ground zero, shopping for T-shirts that say I WILL SURVIVE — instead of aiding with the evacuation of those who won't.

The truth is that we all live in the Red Zone. We have been warned:

"But the Day of the Lord will come like a thief. The heavens will disappear with a roar; the elements will be destroyed by fire, and the earth and everything in it will be laid bare.

"Since everything will be destroyed in this way, what kind of people ought you to be? You ought to live holy and godly lives as you look forward to the day of God and speed its coming. That day will bring about the destruction of the heavens by fire, and the elements will melt in the heat. But in keeping with His promise we are looking forward to a new heaven and a new earth, the home of righteousness.

"So then, dear friends, since you are looking forward to this, make every effort to be found spotless, blameless and at peace with Him" (2 Peter 3:10-14).

None of us will live on this mountain forever. It's going to move, and with a force that will make Mount St. Helens eminently forgettable.

Before it does, I need to remember something. I need to remember that I have friends on this mountain.

That's hard to remember when the earth hasn't started quaking, when the elements haven't melted, when the fire has yet to fall.

But that's the only time remembering will do the slightest bit of good.

Neighbors

I KNEW PERFECTLY WELL who my neighbors
were when I was in high school. A glance through
my bedroom window revealed the Renners' house
next door; through one living room window I
could admire Mrs. Brown's well-trimmed lawn
across Maple; and there, across Hickory, sat the
Williamses and their sprawling garden. From our
corner we could see the whole neighborhood — or
so I thought.

My mother had a different view of who our
neighbors were. Maybe that was because she took
so many walks, usually at the urging of our dog,
Puppy, who one day tugged her past a gloomy,
two-story building three blocks from our house.

It wasn't just the grimy, off-white exterior and

the darkened windows that made this place look so hopeless. It was the people. Some of them sat in the shadows behind the windows, staring at nothing. Some of them wandered aimlessly on the tiny lawn in front. Most of the people were old, but some were younger — mentally or physically broken, apparently judged by someone as beyond repair.

This was not one of those *nice* nursing homes. It was not the kind where social workers led low-impact calesthenics, and volunteers played old favorites on the piano, and relatives came to visit. Mom could see that. And having seen it, she could never return to the next-door and across-the-street definition of our neighborhood again.

Soon she worked up enough courage to step inside that place and ask a few questions of the suspicious woman who managed it. Yes, it was a nursing home. No, it didn't get many visitors. Of course, the Salvation Army marched through at Christmastime with cheery greetings and gift cans of deodorant, but everyone *expected* the Salvation Army to do things like that. Forgotten by relatives and unadopted by any local church, this nursing home and its residents had fallen through the cracks.

That wouldn't have bothered some people, but

it bothered Mom. She knew the answer to the question asked by that lawyer in Luke 10: "Who is my neighbor?" Instead of trying to keep her neighborhood small and manageable, she decided to widen its boundaries.

That December, just before Christmas, she appointed herself a sort of neighbor-at-large. She bought candies and baked sugar cookies, wrapped them in red and green poinsettia paper, and took them to the dingy building three blocks away.

"Well," said a surprised aide, spying Mom's box of presents. "Where are you from?"

"Oh, just down the street," Mom answered.

The woman frowned. "Yes," she said, "but where are you *from?* Who are you *with?*" There had to be an organization, some annual project backing this stranger.

"I'm just a neighbor," Mom said matter-of-factly.

"A *neighbor?*" The aide was dumbfounded. Finally she let Mom in, but watched warily as she handed out her gifts.

The staff also watched her the following Christmas when she returned. They kept watching as she expanded her services to include a homebaked cake and a present for each forgotten resident on his or her birthday. At last they believed her.

We all believed in her too, of course. Dad joined her program early on, helping with the growing load of candies and cookies. But I believed from a distance — agreeing to wrap packages once in a while, but glad to keep three blocks between the nursing home and me. My definition of neighborhood was, after all, the *normal* one.

And so it might have stayed, had I not married a woman whose definitions were open to change.

When our first Christmas together drew near, Liz and I agreed to launch some new family traditions. Collecting quaint copper ornaments was one, but we needed one more: donating money so that someone else could have a happier Christmas. Naturally, we thought of Mom and her project — and handed over enough cash to buy that year's presents.

My warm feelings of charity turned to ice, however, two days before the holiday arrived. "We'll go to the rest home early on Christmas Eve," Liz said casually, as if it had all been discussed.

"We?" I echoed.

"Sure," she said. "Your folks will take a load of

presents in their car, and we'll take one in ours."

This is impossible, I thought. How could I go into that place where the senile people were, the dying ones, the grown men with the minds of pre-schoolers? What if they tried to touch me, or talk to me? And the smells — I could already imagine the smells.

I cleared my throat to protest, but nothing came out. Like that lawyer in Luke 10, I could feel God pulling at the edges of my boundaries. With all my might I pulled back, but already the muscles of my will were starting to ache. I knew that in the end I would have to go.

But I wouldn't have to stretch my boundaries, I told myself. I would go in body only. My mind and heart would stay at home, comfortably watching the twinkling lights on my *real* neighbors' houses.

And so on Christmas Eve I stood in front of the nursing home, shivering from more than the cold. The four of us — Mom, Dad, Liz, and I — held card-board cartons heavy with cookies, candy sticks, and fruit. The fruit had been carefully counted: or-anges and apples for patients with teeth, oranges only for those without.

"Ready?" Dad asked, sounding much too enthused. He opened the door, and stale, musty smells drifted toward us. After reminding myself to stay safely numb, I followed.

The dining room was the size of a living room, crammed with tables and chairs. Several pale figures sat or slumped there, jaws slack, eyes staring at us.

I turned away. In the corner I saw an open guest book lying on a table. Its pages were yellowed. I wondered how long it had been turned to that page, unsigned.

"Well, Mama," my father murmured, "you know your way around." We hefted our boxes and followed her.

Up a rubber-treaded ramp we walked. At the other end we paused in the dim corridor. Mom did a quick mental calculation and pulled from the boxes a bag of oranges, a package of candy sticks, and a few cookies. With these gifts she entered a room halfway down the hall.

Through the doorway I could see an old woman in a chair. Mom bent her head close to the woman's ear. "Merry Christmas, Honey," Mom said. Though there was no response, Mom repeated the greeting, this time more loudly and with a catch in her voice.

We followed Mom into the next room, a larger one full of beds whose blankets were coarse and army-green. A television burbled in the corner, but no one watched it. This was a men's ward, and two of its grizzled occupants sat on their beds and looked up at us.

"Merry Christmas!" Dad said brightly, as if he had just invented the phrase. He handed the men their apples and oranges. Mom gave them cookies, and Liz passed the candy.

"Well," said one of the men, a cynical edge in his voice. "Where are *you* from?"

"Oh, we're just neighbors," my parents replied, almost in unison.

"Neighbors?" the man cried. His face crinkled into a grin. "Well, Merry Christmas!"

Mom took charge again. She surveyed the room, apparently judging the other residents' chewing powers by observing their bedspreads. "Oranges," she directed, pointing at an empty bed. "Apples," she declared, pointing at another. I followed orders, dropping bags of fruit on mattress after mattress. Mom knew these neighbors well, all right.

Suddenly I stood before a bed that was occupied. A little man, disabled in ways I could not guess, lay waiting for his presents. A contorted and perpetual smile was on his face.

"Merry Christmas," my family was saying to him. He could not speak or even hold his packages, but even I could read his smiling eyes.

"Merry Christmas," someone said in a small voice. All at once I realized it was me.

My boundaries were slipping. I tried, but I couldn't keep my grip on them. Slowly they stretched with each sack of fruit I dispensed, with each grateful nod I received.

They stretched again in the next room, where a big, bald man crossed to his corner to find something. At the top of her voice Mom called him by name; they had been neighbors ever since her visits began.

"He wants to take our picture," Mom said. We all stood and smiled, and the flashcube flashed.

"Merry Christmas," we said.

"God bless you," he said softly to Mom.

At last we reached the dining room. We had come full circle; it was time to go.

"Merry Christmas," Mom called out.

A stooped, white-haired woman emerged from the crowd of patients and moved toward Mom. The woman's eyes were clouded, confused.

"What?" the woman cried, the simple word twisting in her throat. "What?"

"Merry Christmas," Mom repeated, her gaze reaching out to the woman who continued to totter forward.

"What?" cried the woman again. Her face was urgent, fearful, lost.

"Merry Christmas," breathed my mother, tears in her voice. She caught the woman in her arms and held her, held her until the urgency and fear and lostness melted away. "Merry Christmas," Mom whispered once more.

It was hard to say our Merry Christmases now, but we did. We moved toward the door. As we stepped outside, I heard an aide explaining something to a patient.

"Look what the neighbors brought," she was saying loudly. "The neighbors."

Neighbors. As I walked to the car, saying it to myself, it sounded like a brand new word. And in a way, it was.

*   *   *   *

Years have passed, and that nursing home is closed now. Its patients have been parceled out to

133

other homes in other places, other neighbor-
hoods. I can't help but wonder who their neighbors are now.

Who *is* my neighbor? And yours?

Blest Be the Ties

ONCE IN A GREAT WHILE, a group of thoroughly likeminded Christians is drawn together — a group so much in agreement, so naturally harmonious, with so much in common, that nothing can pull it apart.

This was not one of those times.

I could see it as I looked around the large living room where we were meeting. This group Liz and I had recently become part of, this thing that called itself The Community, could not possibly last.

The people were just too different from each other. They gave new meaning to the term *grab bag*. How could they ever stick together?

Sitting by the coffee table was John — the other John — the rail-thin, bearded son of a missionary to

China. John was a prophet, ascetic and intense as his baptizing namesake. In the armchair was Bill—rugby enthusiast, lover of fine foods and art, a counselor by profession. He was big and burly with a booming voice—the opposite of John.

On the couch sat Murna. Stout and feisty, middle-aged, she was the antithesis of Jim, who sat nearby. Jim was soft-voiced, melancholy, self-deprecating. Surely Murna's no-nonsense, quit-whining approach would someday drive Jim away.

Then there was Bob, blond hair to his shoulders, a sly, funky philosopher and guitar player who seemed to know but not care that the 1960s had ended seven years before. He couldn't have been more different from the balding Roger, perhaps the oldest member of the group, a respected elder in a large church, teacher in a Christian school, father of several children.

The whole room was full of mismatches: brooding, questioning Tim and outgoing, arm-waving Lynn; peaceful flower child Tess, and rapid-fire idea man Ralph; huggy, Pentecostal Kathi, and restrained, undemonstrative me.

No way could this group make it. It was an experiment that had to fail.

But somehow that didn't matter to those of us sitting around the room that night. There seemed to be an unspoken understanding among us: We had to try to make this work.

Some felt that way because they'd tried everything else. Disappointed with the "organized church," they wanted one last shot at forming a fellowship like the one they'd read about in the New Testament. Others were intrigued with the idea of community, having heard of Christians who'd set up communes; they wanted to see whether that kind of relationship could be created without having to share a building. Still others were there because they had nowhere else to go. They were too needy, too different, or too full of doubts to fit most churches in our town.

So there we were, an unmatched set of malcontents, burnouts, zealots, seekers, and idealists. We knew we had to try to make a go of things, but how? What could keep us together long enough to make it work?

We didn't know. So we began to do the only thing we could think of: spending time together. As much time as we could. Doing things sacred, secular, and somewhere in between.

We stood side by side one afternoon, hammers in our hands, knocking holes in the old plaster walls of John's basement so he could try building a halfway house there. We crowded around Bill's TV to watch new shows called "60 Minutes" and "Saturday Night Live." We ate countless meals together, shared recipes for taco salad, and stood in long, slow lines for *Star Wars.*

We showed each other things we'd made — a wooden planter, slides of national parks, a handcrafted dulcimer. We told each other about our jobs, what we hated, what we liked, what we someday hoped to be.

In meetings we taught each other new songs, studied the Bible, and laughed at group members' babies who made faces and played peekaboo. After meetings we hung around for hours, probing and philosophizing, joking and commiserating, wondering and trying to answer.

Soon something strange began to happen in the group. Somehow all these people who couldn't possibly have gotten along were getting along. Not perfectly, but consistently. Something mysterious was bringing us together, linking us.

It was visible in the meetings as well as out.

When we shared needs and news it was unforced, without the testimony-time strain so many of us had grown up with. When we prayed for each other, it was in detail and with feeling—and expectantly, because we knew we'd be around to see the outcome.

In time our numbers grew. People seemed attracted by this odd assortment of Christians who somehow got along.

Some asked what our secret was. No one seemed to know, exactly. Perhaps there was no single answer.

But during one of our retreats I found a Scripture passage that seemed, at least to me, to hold a clue.

We were at a picnic area in the woods, looking at copies of Ephesians 4, underlining parts we thought applied to our life together. I came to verses 15 and 16:

"But speaking the truth in love, we are to grow up in all aspects into Him, who is the head, even Christ, from whom the whole body, being fitted and held together *by that which every joint supplies,* according to the proper working of each individual part, causes the growth of the body for the building up of itself in love" (NASB, italics added).

139

By that which every joint supplies. Puzzled, I underlined the phrase. It was new to me — the phrase and the idea.

How could one joint — one person — hold a body together? I'd thought Christians were held together from the top, as if God were wrapping His arms around them and squeezing. Sort of forcing them to stick together. I'd never really seen it work, but I'd thought it was supposed to.

But this phrase said something different. *By that which every joint supplies.* Every joint, every individual, was to supply something. Secrete it, like a gland. Something that would ultimately hold the whole body together.

What was this something?

Glue, I guessed. A sort of spiritual glue.

Just a little bit of glue, joining each person to those on this side and that side, and if everyone supplied his or her bit of glue, the whole body would be joined so strongly that it would have time to grow.

And that, I realized, was why The Community was sticking together. Each person was producing just enough glue to bond himself or herself to the next person. All that time spent together, all those taco salads, all those conversations and jokes and sessions of trying to tune our guitars to the same notes were yielding one-to-one relationships that bonded the whole group.

No one person could supply enough glue to cement the whole body. But no one person had to. If we stayed so involved in each other's lives, there would be just enough glue to go around.

It seemed so simple. I wondered why I'd never seen that passage before—in the Bible, or in practice.

Maybe it was because I'd never spent so much time making taco salad, standing in line at the movies, and giving people rides when their cars broke down. Maybe I'd never had guests over when the whole house was a mess, or risked singing a song I'd just written, or admitted that I felt lousy sometimes even though I had eternal life.

Or maybe I'd just never looked around at the motley crew of Christians I happened to be sitting with, decided there was no way it could work— and tried anyway.

*   *   *   *

I wish I could say I never forgot that truth from Ephesians 4. But in time the group's web of relationships seemed inadequate to me; we needed structure to survive, I said. Unless the group became more of a church, I predicted, it would never hold together.

When nothing changed, I left. Liz left with me, wisely grieving more than I the loss of those relationships.

The group survived, despite my dire warnings. We did too but always with an empty place in our hearts. The Community became our Christian Camelot — a place where, for one brief, shining moment, we knew what it was like to be as close as brothers and sisters were meant to be.

Today we're far away from The Community — 2,000 miles and a dozen years. I miss every face from those days, every minute we spent together, every meal we ate, every prayer we prayed.

But maybe, instead of pining for the past, I could apply it. Maybe I could find one person, or two or three, in my present church — and start to knit my little corner of that body together. Who knows what might happen?

Anybody could do that. In any church, anywhere.

All it takes is a little glue.

A Wilderness Diary

DAY 1: WHY ARE YOU DOING THIS TO ME?

After months of looking for a job, I finally landed one. As You know, it started today.

And what kind of job is it?

Well, what kind *should* a guy with a bachelor's degree in communications and English — plus experience in journalism and public relations — get?

And if that guy has decided he really wants to go into full-time Christian work, what kind of position *should* he have?

Wrong! As of today, I'm punching cash register buttons and stocking shelves in a discount store!

What are You trying to do to me?

Oh, it's not like the job doesn't have its perks. I get to wear a one-size-fits-nobody red store jacket with a name tag. I get to make a few cents above minimum wage. I get to mingle with fellow employees whose ambition is to save up enough to buy a new pair of fuzzy dice to hang from their rearview mirrors!

Thank You so much! During all those months that I scoured the want ads in the middle of a recession, during all those times I got turned down for jobs because I was "overqualified," I knew You'd come through for me someday.

You finally found something I'm qualified for: sticking price tags on cheap glassware!

All right, I'm sorry.

But You know how I feel.

You know how, after that budget cut ended my last job, I thought long and hard about what to do with my life. You remember the day I sat in my car in that parking lot, thinking about the value of working for You.

I thought about my parents, how being a pastor and pastor's wife had been so intense and fulfilling for them. I thought about Mr. Fairley at church, and other retired missionaries I've seen. And I wanted to be like them.

See, I want to make sure that when I get to the

end of my life, I won't feel like I've wasted it. I want to do the most important work there is.

Your work, right?

So why am I working as a clerk in a discount store? Why have You stuck me in the wilderness?

DAY 2: It's bad enough to have a second-rate — You know, secular — job. But this is *third*-rate — a *lousy* secular job!

The manager of the Variety department makes it even worse. Here I am a college graduate, probably several dozen I.Q. points above him, and he calls me "Hoss" — as though I were a beast of burden or the big, dumb Cartwright son on the old "Bonanza" TV series.

He also calls me "Chief." I'll be on my knees in the aisle, juggling cans of tennis balls from one rack to another, and he'll say, "How ya doin', Chief?" I figure it's a reference to that big, silent Indian guy who always swept the floor of the insane asylum in the movie *One Flew over the Cuckoo's Nest*.

What a lovely comparison. Is that how I look in my little red jacket as I dust shelves and haul empty cardboard cartons to the crusher?

How could You put me in this position?

145

What's that? You say I have a little to learn about humility?

Well, isn't *that* nice?

DAY 6: I'm done with in-store training. Four years of college, and I had a terrible time learning how to use a cash register.

I also learned what to say to customers. And what to do about shoplifters.

I didn't think I'd ever come face to face with a shoplifter myself. But today I did, and it gave me something to think about.

It happened when I waited on a guy from church. He looked pale as he brought a small purchase — a screwdriver, I think — to my check-out. He looked even paler when he saw me.

As soon as he paid and walked out, a deter-mined-looking blonde ran up to my checkout and yanked the chain across the aisle to close it. She was a store detective.

"Look out for the guy you just waited on," she said. "Shoplifter. We've seen him take little things before, but he always puts them back when he re-alizes he's being watched.

"If he comes in here again, let me know," she

ordered. "Next time we're going to nail him."

I swallowed as she walked away. *But I know that guy,* I thought. *He's a Christian.*

I started praying for him, right then. It was just a quick prayer before the next customer came along. But it *was* a prayer — something I didn't think I'd be doing much of in this job.

It was weird to see that guy revealed as a shoplifter. It was almost as weird to see spiritual stuff leaking into this "secular" place.

I'm not sure what it all means.

DAY 14: Today I got a great assignment — cleaning out the Layaway and Return bins in the back of the store.

What a filthy job! Everything was covered with dust and grime. Every carton in the huge bins seemed to be in the wrong place, and it was my task to sort them alphabetically and cull out those that had been unclaimed for too long.

Was I chosen because I'm the only employee who knows the alphabet? Or because the manager wanted to see "Hoss" get his hands dirty?

Or were You behind this one?

I was tempted not to do a thorough job. It would

have been so easy to leave the boxes that were too far back in the bin or too hard to lift. But I remembered a story about an old house painter who always painted the hard-to-get places, like up in the eaves.

"Why waste your time painting there?" somebody asked him. "People can't see it."

"But God can," the old man said, and kept painting.

So, do You? Do You see the Layaway and Return bins? And if so, do You care whether they're clean and alphabetized?

I ended up doing a good job, if I say so myself. Nobody complimented me on it, so I hope You're pleased.

The more I do this job, the more I think about the verse that says to do all things as unto the Lord. And the verse about whatsoever your hand finds to do, do it with all your might.

I must be getting desperate.

Or maybe I'm learning something.

But this is only temporary, right?

Hello?

DAY 20: Today I noticed something interesting about the store.

There are all these *people* in it.

They keep coming in to buy things. We employees can try to ignore them, pretending to be busy with our price guns and shelf hooks, or we can try to serve them.

The company wants us to do more than that, of course. We're supposed to get people to buy things they didn't plan to — "meeting the customer's hidden needs," it's called.

Those may be phony needs, but there are an awful lot of real needs here too.

Take the other day. A man and woman came in. It didn't take me long to figure out they were mentally disabled. They also didn't know where anything was.

Their words were slow, garbled. They'd point at things and ask questions, and I'd have no idea what they were saying. I was concentrating so hard on trying to understand them that my head was pounding.

So I asked for Your help. Finally I figured out what they wanted, and their smiles made the battle worthwhile.

There have been others too. I've waited on deaf customers, carrying on a notepad conversation.

149

I've waited on people who nearly suffocated me with their body odor. I've waited and waited on customers who took forever to decide.

Each of them needed something I could give: service. This whole servant thing is a little new to me.

But not to You, I suppose.

DAY 29: Something *very* weird happened today.

I was at the register when a young woman walked up. She placed on the counter a small box of gold stick-on stars.

Punching the CASH button on the register, I glanced at her. A sort of chill came over me. She looked normal enough, but there was something about her that made me feel uncomfortable.

I felt compelled to ask her a question. "Gold stars, huh? What are you planning to use them for, if I might ask?"

Her reply was matter-of-fact: "We're going to have a black sabbath."

I paused. Maybe she was kidding, but her expression seemed to say otherwise. I'd heard five-pointed stars — pentagrams — were used in satanic rituals. But little gold stars, bought at a discount store?

I decided to take her at her word. "In that case," I said, "I'm sorry to be selling them to you."

She wasn't very happy about that. Taking her change, she marched off with her purchase.

Whether she was really headed for a black sabbath or not, the incident made me think. In the big spiritual battle, where are the front lines? In church? At a cash register? Or both?

You're trying to tell me something, aren't You?

DAY 40: Customers aren't the only ones around here who need help. The lives of some employees are falling apart.

One of the clerks, a single woman, has just discovered she's pregnant. She doesn't know whether the guy will marry her.

Other employees are slowly being ground to bits by the low pay and unpredictable work schedules. They hate their jobs, and the evening-and-weekend hours keep them from being with their families.

They're trapped here, it seems. But I'm not.

It turns out that a one-year internship is opening up at my church. If I take it, I'll have a chance to find out how my college degree might be used in church work.

It's not a hard decision to make. But it's not as clear-cut as it would have been forty days ago.

While I've been wandering in the wilderness, wishing for the Promised Land, something happened. Somebody erased the line between spiritual and secular, and I can't find it anymore.

Somebody showed me that a life lived for You — in a store or under a steeple — is a life never regretted.

Not paying more attention to people, not making the most of every opportunity, not accepting Your choices — those are the things a person comes to regret.

I know I already do.

DAY 45: My final day. I'm taking the internship.

I walked around the store before I left, looking at things and people for the last time. I took off my red jacket and badge and turned them in.

I wonder who'll wear that jacket next.

Somebody who thinks he's too good for the wilderness?

Or somebody who's willing to be Your trainee?

DLB

ONE OF THE GREATEST TEACHERS I've ever
known is Donald L. Bubna.

That probably would come as no surprise to
those who've heard of him. A lot of people
have — about as many as can hear of a Christian
leader who doesn't have a TV show, a radio program, a megachurch, or a string of bestsellers. A
pastor for decades in California, Oregon, and Brit-
ish Columbia, Don crisscrosses the globe, speaking to ministers and missionaries. He's a respected
statesman in the Christian and Missionary Alliance,
an author, a contributing editor for *Leadership*
journal, a world-class church administrator.

And a great teacher.

Calling Don a great teacher certainly would

come as no surprise to those who've heard him preach. I can still remember sitting as a teenager in the vast and crowded Salem Alliance Church sanctuary in Salem, Oregon, watching Pastor Bubna do what he seemed born to do. Wired for sound, he would ignore the pulpit, stationing and restationing himself all over the platform, seemingly determined to deliver his message face-to-face with each of the several hundred people present. Yet his voice was calm, matter-of-fact as he explained the Scripture from angle after angle, adding real-life analogies until all of us could feel the texture of invisible things like forgiveness and eternity. Then, near the end of almost every sermon, he would plant his feet firmly, stretch out his arm, and his voice would rise from earnest discourse to ringing declaration—and we would all know exactly which piece of God's unchangeable truth we needed to apply that week.

I've never seen so many people take sermon notes as I did when Pastor Bubna preached—and with good reason.

Calling Don a great teacher would also come as no surprise to those who've served as church interns under his supervision. I did that after college, tagging along behind the man whose church was now serving 1,500. One couldn't help but learn from DLB, as he was known around the church office. He explained the value of rehearsing sermons in the empty sanctuary on Saturday, shared his thoughts on serving Communion, discussed how to introduce new ideas without splitting a congregation. He hauled us along as he visited shut-ins, as he encouraged pastors from smaller churches, as he poured oil on the troubled waters of an elders' disagreement. Each Wednesday in staff meeting he demonstrated how to plan a worship service, hovering over timed-to-the-minute blueprints for the coming Sunday. And he reminded us of the limits of planning when, at the ends of those meetings, he would lace his fingers behind his head and humbly paraphrase Proverbs 21:31: "The horse is made ready for battle, but victory belongs to the Lord."

I learned more that year about how churches are supposed to work than I have in all the other years of my life. All the members of the staff contributed to that, but I owe the lion's share to DLB.

Yet when I say Don Bubna is one of the greatest teachers I've ever known, I don't just mean Donald

L. Bubna, globetrotting speaker. Or Pastor Bubna, gifted preacher. Or DLB, mentor to the up-and-coming.

I'm also describing just plain Don, the man who teaches even without meaning to. The one who keeps shining light on other people simply by being who he is.

I've seen him do it many times.

* * * *

Like the time Liz and I, newly married, decided to try our hands at hospitality. We invited over several young adults from church, plus one older couple: Pastor Bubna and his wife Dee.

We wanted everything to go perfectly, especially since Pastor Bubna would be there. The evening would begin with pizza; then we'd all go to a performance of the play *Godspell*, the rock musical based loosely on Matthew's Gospel.

The big night arrived. The young adults and the Bubnas crammed into our little apartment, sitting on borrowed chairs. Liz and I bustled happily in the kitchen, knowing no more about cooking than we did about nuclear fusion.

Our hearts were light, but alas, our crust was

not. The overbaked pizzas resembled the tiles of a space shuttle, capable of cracking teeth. Mortified, we crunched and gnawed with our guests, waiting for the chance to redeem the evening later at the theater.

Unfortunately, *Godspell* turned out to be as indigestible as our pizza — at least to a careful Bible expositor like Pastor Bubna. For two hours he watched actors jump around in garish costumes and clown makeup and pretend to be Jesus and His disciples. By the time the play was over, our senior pastor looked as if he'd just seen an all-nude version of *Pilgrim's Progress.*

Looking at the pained expression on Pastor Bubna's face, I was sure our stab at hospitality was a total loss. I braced for an exhortation about the sacred and the profane, or at least a few words on the importance of staying true to the New Testament account. Instead, Don graciously thanked us for the pizza and said with sincerity and effort that the play had been "thought-provoking."

It may have been a small thing, what Don did that night. But it loomed large to me. He'd accepted our hospitality, however flawed, and in so doing he'd accepted us. It showed me something

Don already knew: In the kingdom of God it was more important to be an encourager than a critic.

* * * *

Then there was the time my internship was ending, and I seemed headed for a brick wall. Unlike most other interns, I wasn't aiming for a pulpit or a mission field; all I had was a degree in communications and a vague desire to work for some kind of Christian organization. The specifics were a mystery, and I had no clues.

DLB had an idea. For months I'd been drawing overhead transparencies for his sermons and designing posters and brochures. Maybe I could keep creating graphics for the church part time, he said, and free lance the rest of the week. There was a storage room upstairs in the church, and I could work there.

But even a part-time salary took money, and no slack could be found in the church budget. Instead of shrugging and wishing me a fond farewell, Don kept trying. He knew I loved to draw, and he loved the church, and he wanted the church and me to stay together.

He suggested I do free work for the church in exchange for the upstairs room. But he also put his money where his words were. He and Dee gave me $90 — their own, not the church's — so that I could buy a drawing table.

I'd never had a drawing table, not a real one. The one I bought with that money was a beauty — solid, made all of wood, stained maple brown with a hardwood top hand-rubbed with oil.

It was more than a place to draw. It was concrete proof of Don's belief that there was more to come, that God would complete in me the work He had begun.

I still have that drawing table, fifteen years and 2,000 miles from that storage room. I've illustrated eight books on its elegant surface. Every time I set a sheet of paper on it, I remember where it came from — and how Don taught me that faith is proved not by words, but by things you can see and spend and touch.

*   *   *   *

And of course there was the time I visited Salem Alliance Church one Easter morning, having moved away to Illinois several years before. I looked forward to seeing Don again, to seeing one of his perfectly planned, smoothly running services.

I slipped into the swiftly filling sanctuary, gazing around at the familiar red-padded pews and the walls of warm Pacific Northwest wood. The memories were palpable — memories of Pastor Bubna standing on that platform, of standing knock-kneed on it myself. Memories of kids from the youth group, and of people no longer here or in any earthly congregation — like Jess Kaufman, the longtime board member who had suffered for at least a year with cancer before dying just months ago.

The organ music started, and crescendoed, and the service was underway. Soon there was Don, standing near the pulpit, looking just the way I remembered him, ready to take charge of the proceedings he'd planned so carefully.

But when Don began to speak, it was clear that I was not the only one who'd been remembering. In a halting voice he explained how, every year on Easters just like this, his friend Jess Kaufman would arrive early at the church and call out a joyous Resurrection greeting: "He is risen!"

Don would always counter, "As He said!"

And now, trying to call out the greeting and reply, Don Bubna's voice broke, and the tears came. He wept there on the platform, missing his friend whose voice he would not hear again until heaven.

The service stopped, suspended — the service planned by DLB, begun by Pastor Bubna, but brought down to earth by Don. Brought down to earth by his transparency, by his willingness to let us see the bittersweet truth that even though Christ's resurrection was history, ours was yet to come.

It took a minute for him, and for the rest of us, to dry our eyes. But in that minute the most powerful message of the morning had already been declared. Everyone in the sanctuary knew it was all right to let your guard down, to mourn even when rejoicing would come soon. It was all right to weep, whether your friend was Lazarus or Jess, to cause others to say, "See how He loved him!" (John 11:36) It was all right to be so transparent that the light could shine right through you.

I'd seen the light through Don many times, but that Easter morning he glowed most brightly. Even more brightly than when he preached, even more than when he advised and demonstrated and tutored in the church office. Somehow all the things I'd learned from him rang truer after that, coming as they did from one who'd turned out to be so real, so human.

*　*　*　*

That's why Donald L. Bubna is one of the greatest teachers I've ever known. It's how he taught me that great teaching doesn't require a platform or a position; it takes qualities like grace, generosity, genuineness.

And a willingness to let the light shine, even when you hadn't planned on it.

Anybody could be that kind of teacher. Even those of us who, having known great teachers like Don Bubna, still have so much left to learn.

His Eye Is on the Sparrow

IT HAD BEEN ONE OF THOSE NIGHTS.

I'd spent most of it lying awake in bed, holding my wife's hand. She was awake too — sick with stomach cramps. We knew they'd eventually go away, but until they did Liz would suffer. Every so often she'd cry in pain, and I'd silently ask, *Lord, please help her feel better*.

The prayers didn't work. With every cry from Liz my feeling of helplessness grew. There was nothing I could do. There was plenty God could do; why didn't He just do it?

Even in the middle of the night I knew all the standard replies to that question:

• God always answers prayer, but sometimes He says no, or wait.

- We suffer because we live in a fallen world.
- God doesn't erase evil from the earth because He'd have to erase us too.
- We grow stronger through difficulty.
- Everything will be fine — someday.

They were perfectly good answers — at noon on a sunny day, when your wife wasn't groaning in pain at your side. But at 1:30 A.M. in the dark, all I wanted was for God to at least notice that something miserable was going on in this obscure corner of His kingdom.

I stopped praying and watched the minutes tick by on the clock radio. As the glowing numbers slowly replaced each other, I wondered whether God really did keep an eye on things like this — matters of less than life and death. He *could,* I knew, but *did* He? Maybe the world was so messed up that only major crises — rivers cresting at flood stage, souls teetering on the edge of conversion — were enough to trip the alarm in heaven.

Maybe the old hymn was wrong:
His eye is on the sparrow,
And I know He watches me.

Maybe those Bible verses about God seeing the sparrows fall weren't meant to be taken literally.

I knew that sounded heretical, but I hadn't seen anything to contradict it. Especially not tonight. Too tired to think any more, I closed my eyes and waited for Liz's pain to subside. Finally it did, around 3 A.M.

At 5:30 A.M. the clock radio buzzed us awake. It was time for Liz to go to work broadcasting news at a local radio station. Dutifully she got up and left, even though it was Saturday, even though her stomach still ached.

When I got up a couple of hours later, the night's doubts clung to me like stale, secondhand smoke. Was God watching? Did He care?

I didn't know it, but I was about to find out.

Frowning, I went outside and lugged the lawn mower from the garage. The backyard needed trimming, and I'd have nothing else to do until Liz dragged herself home that afternoon.

Leaving the mower at the edge of the tall grass, I scanned the yard for rocks and sticks that might get caught in the blade. Suddenly I noticed something—in the shade of our backyard's only tree.

It was a baby bird, about three inches long. Its gray-brown feathers were flecked with soft, white down. I didn't know what kind of bird it was, but I knew it was in trouble.

At first there was no movement. Then I saw the tiny black eyes blink, and the little chest rise and fall.

"Hey, little bird," I said, rustling the grass with my fingers. He didn't budge.

Maybe he fell out of his nest, I thought, examining the tree overhead. But no nest was visible.

I straightened up, stymied. I couldn't mow the lawn with this little creature quivering in the middle of it. Nudging him gently again, I watched as he let out a screech, fluttered his wings, and hopped a few feet.

Just then a loud chorus of chirps and warbles filled the air. I looked up to see two or three larger birds perched on a nearby power line, with more on the back fence. Two of them — a male and female, judging by their coloring — seemed louder and more interested than the rest.

The parents, I thought. If I could get the baby to screech and hop again, maybe they'd spot him and come to his rescue.

But another nudge from my finger merely sent the little bird stumbling in the wrong direction —

away from the others. Still chirping, he took refuge on the sill of a basement window and refused to move.

I sighed. I could mow the lawn now, making sure to steer clear of the window sill. But this bird was not long for this world. He'd starve — unless a neighborhood cat got him first.

Reaching down, I yanked the mower to life. The congress of birds kept up its filibuster as I cut the grass. A pitiful peep sounded regularly from the windowsill.

An hour later I was done. Carrying the empty grass catcher into the darkness of the garage, I wondered what would happen to the little bird.

I'd tried to help. What else could I do? Pray?

No way, I thought. That would be ridiculous, praying for a bird. Hadn't I just spent half the night praying for my wife, only to be disappointed? After that, why would I pray for a bird?

Yet there he was, tiny and defenseless and still chirping weakly on the window sill. And that verse about falling sparrows was still in the Bible.

It was almost as if Somebody had set this up. *Go ahead,* He seemed to be saying. *You'll have to trust Me about last night. But this morning, test Me.*

167

I wasn't sure about the trusting, but I was in the mood for a test. That sort of thing was normally discouraged, I knew—but this time I'd practically gotten an engraved invitation.

So I prayed for the bird. It was a short prayer, a request that God would somehow get him back together with his parents. It felt silly, but it was sincere.

Returning to the backyard for the mower, I glanced at the basement window sill. The baby bird was still there. *Sure enough,* I thought, *nothing's going to happen.*

But all at once, as if on cue, things changed.

The little bird jumped off the sill and hopped back into the grass, this time in the right direction.

The chirping from his "parents" grew louder and louder. They flew into the branches of the tree.

I watched, openmouthed, as the baby hopped under the tree, cried loudly, and headed for the back fence. One of the parents swooped down and began poking its beak at the little one's in a feeding motion. It looked like the reunion of the prodigal son and his father.

Eventually my neighbor, Jim, discovered me

standing there. He must have wondered why I was staring at a bunch of birds on the ground.

"Hey," Jim said. "What are you looking for, worms?"

I told him what had happened — except for the part about the prayer. I was still too embarrassed to mention that.

"Well, I'll be," Jim said, leaning on his rake. "Sounds like the same little sparrow the lady across the street found under *their* tree last night. She was all worried about it."

A *sparrow?* As if I might have missed the point, a genuine sparrow had been included in this object lesson. A sparrow whose fall had not gone unnoticed.

I watched as the larger birds guarded their flightless baby, ready to swoop down on any cat who dared enter their territory. Chances were good that the little bird — the little sparrow — would be all right.

And chances were excellent that next time I had questions for God, I'd be a little more willing to take Him at His Word.

Not that I would stop asking, or that the answers would be easy to swallow. Especially in the middle of the night. Especially when I couldn't have all the truth I wanted.

But for now I'd seen enough to keep me going.

"Are not two sparrows sold for a penny? Yet not one of them will fall to the ground apart from the will of your Father. . . . So don't be afraid; you are worth more than many sparrows" (Matt. 10:29, 31).

The Immersion

UNTIL THE MORNING I saw Chantal take the plunge, I'd never quite figured out this whole baptism thing.

Not that baptism had been a mystery to me. Quite the contrary. I knew Mark 16:16 and the story of the Ethiopian eunuch too. I'd been baptized myself at age twelve. I'd seen dozens of people symbolically buried and resurrected in rivers and tanks of all dimensions and depths. But when I watched them step into that water, something in my attitude was naggingly askew.

Somehow I couldn't feel what others seemed to feel about this ordinance. I couldn't drum up the awe, the first-day-of-the-rest-of-your-life exhilaration, the sense of clouds parting and doves descending.

I saw baptism as a duty—and a funny-looking one at that.

My baptism had felt that way. It had been a perfectly effective immersion, performed by my pastor father in another church's borrowed baptistery—our own little building being unsuitably plumbed. I'd spent the previous eight years itching to get the watery ordeal over with, having prayed at age four to receive Jesus as my Savior.

On my baptismal afternoon the unfamiliar sanctuary was almost empty. I emerged from the dressing room, clad in a thin, white robe, and stepped barefoot into a small cement pool. After answering the usual faith-affirming questions, I held my breath as Dad invoked the Persons of the Trinity. I was submerged, hauled up, and it was over.

Dripping as I made my way back to the dressing room, I'd felt relieved. I'd finally gotten it over with. I'd finally taken care of Part Two of the great believe-and-be-baptized transaction. There was relief, but no euphoria.

Maybe that was why I'd come to see baptism as a duty—just one more thing to get out of the way, like memorizing the books of the Bible or washing all those tiny cups after Communion.

Once I'd done my baptismal duty, it was hard to work up much emotion about others doing theirs. It was also hard to take their dunkings seriously, since the process looked so funny.

No one admitted it out loud, of course, but I knew baptism looked bizarre. People looked ridiculous wading into the water, sloshing and shivering, trying to smile as if they hoped to do this every week. They looked odd standing up to their belt buckles in a tank, conversing about theology, bravely attempting to look as though it were perfectly normal. They looked comical squeezing their eyes shut and falling back into the water, only to be dredged up coughing and sputtering and with their hair in their eyes — all on purpose, all in front of an audience.

And in those churches whose baptisteries were set above the choir loft, people looked funny standing in a little window, visible only from the waist up, chatting away — like puppets in a show.

I couldn't help it. That's how I thought of baptism. It was a funny-looking duty that some people found deeply significant and moving.

Some people, but not me.

Until the morning I saw Chantal take the plunge.

173

I didn't know it was going to happen that Sunday morning. But our friends Bill and Lelia did, and when I saw them sitting several pews behind me I knew something was up. They attended a different church, and only an event of major importance could have brought them here.

Opening the bulletin, I read that Chantal was going to be baptized toward the end of the service.

No wonder Bill and Lelia were here.

For a year Liz and I had been praying with Bill and Lelia that Chantal would come to know Christ. We'd prayed about her almost every time our small home Bible study got together.

Bill had been trying, in his usual low-key way, to tell Chantal about the Lord. A dentist, Bill was used to talking about God with many of the patients who sat in his chair. His new assistant, Chantal, had started listening to those conversations. The more we prayed, the more interested she seemed in hearing — or overhearing — about Jesus.

But then she'd stopped, apparently no longer curious about the Good News. Bill would bring up the subject, but she would let it drop.

"Please pray for Chantal," Bill and Lelia would say at our meetings, their brows furrowed.

For months Chantal topped our list of prayer requests. For months Bill and Lelia's concern deepened as Chantal faced one personal crisis after another. Her boyfriend left; her car died; there was conflict in her family.

And then it happened, after a year of praying. One morning Chantal came to work with an announcement that stunned her dentist boss.

"I did what the book said!" she declared, referring to the Four Spiritual Laws booklet Bill had given her. The previous night she'd read it — and finally had let Christ take the throne of her life.

When our group heard the news, we cheered. Chantal moved from the Prayer Request side to the Praise side of our ledger. Soon she was attending the church Liz and I called home, and it was a pleasure at last to meet the shy, smiling, blond-haired seeker.

And now, just a few months later, she was about to be baptized.

Sitting in the pew and waiting for that event, I found myself feeling something strange. Something I'd never felt before on such occasions.

It was excitement.

It seemed impossible, but this morning I was

175

forgetting everything I thought I'd known about tanks and pools and puppet shows and duty. It was almost as if I'd never seen a baptism before, as if I'd only heard about them and had always wanted to see one.

I wanted the rest of the service to end so that the baptism could begin. My adrenaline was pumping, my heart rate climbing, over nothing more than someone else's wading in the water.

I could almost hear the hearts of Bill and Lelia thumping several rows behind me too. I could imagine their faces bright with parental pride, eager to see their spiritual daughter take her first steps in public. How much they'd invested — all that love and despair, all those careful words, all those dogged requests for prayer. I was proud of Bill and Lelia, and proud to have had a microscopic part in all of this.

Today was no day for words like *ritual* and *awkward.* It was time for celebration, the grand finale of the struggle for Chantal. It was time for the victory party we'd all hoped and prayed for. It was time to see the results in a tangible way, a way as real as flesh and bone — and water.

Finally our wait was over, and the moment arrived. Pastor Richardson took his place in the baptistery and invited us all to come forward to witness the event, as was the custom in our church. We crowded toward the front, and the closer we got the faster my heart drum-rolled.

The pastor stretched his hand out, and Chantal, beaming, took it as she stepped into the water.

He asked the question, the most important question in the world, and still beaming she said yes, Jesus was indeed her Savior and Lord.

"Then, Chantal, I baptize you in the name of the Father, and of the Son, and of the Holy Spirit."

She seemed to fall backward in slow motion into the water. She sank from sight.

And then she bobbed back up, full of irrepressible life.

"Whoooooooooo!" she shouted, and grinned through the water that streamed down her face. It was a whoop of joy, a victory holler, and it took us all by surprise.

We laughed then, the whole congregation, and I laughed even though my view of Chantal was blurred by tears.

Words like *duty* seemed so far away now, with the laughter rebounding in that sanctuary, with

177

the smiling young woman in the white robe making her soggy way back up the baptistry stairs. If she looked silly, it didn't matter. Celebrations, victory parties, usually looked that way.

When the service was all over, I turned and found my way to Bill and Lelia. They stood staring at the empty baptistry, their faces streaked by signs of weeping.

I shook Bill's hand. "This is a pretty special day," I managed to say before my voice gave out completely.

"Yes, it is," he quavered, and then his voice quit.

But that was all right, because Chantal had said it all.

With her hoot of celebration she'd made it clear, even to me, what baptism was about. It was a sign of winning, of one kingdom beating the other kingdom one soul at a time. It was about being on the side that couldn't lose. It was about the end of a fight and the beginning of a lifelong battle that would one day have us all yelling *Worthy is the Lamb!* at the top of our lungs and maybe even looking silly as we did it.

I'd never seen baptism that way before. Not until I was immersed — in the struggle for Chantal.

The James Rap

OK, SO I'M A BIT OF A PERFECTIONIST.

I see the value of maintaining quality control over the projects I'm involved with, that's all. I merely prefer to do things correctly myself instead of entrusting them to the SLOPPY, UNSKILLED, LETHARGIC, HABITUALLY LATE HALFWITS WHO INHABIT 99 PERCENT OF THIS PLANET!!!

Excuse me.

I think I'm all right now.

As I was saying, my natural tendency is to do things decently and in order — and all by myself.

So it must have been God's sense of humor that led Him to saddle me with a class of high school boys — Dan and Joel and Adam and Matt. I was their Sunday School teacher, and they were my dedicated physical therapists. By that I mean they faithfully stretched and pummeled me each week, twisting my expectations and straining my assumptions — especially the belief that I could make things turn out the way I wanted them to.

No matter how carefully I prepared for Sunday mornings, things never happened as I'd planned. If I tried to start on time, Dan would insist that we spend the first few minutes watching the video monitor in the corner of the room, singing along with the opening theme of "The Brady Bunch." If I needed a volunteer to read aloud a key Scripture passage, Joel would do it — leaving out every other word and giggling uncontrollably. If I opened my mouth to deliver a solemn challenge for the coming week, Adam and his younger brother Matt would launch into a shoulder-punching fight — after which Matt would wrinkle up his nose and ask, "Is it time to go yet?"

That was the problem with teaching, I told myself as I picked up crumpled worksheets and far-flung pencils after class each week. *There had to be students.* Had I been the only person in the room, things would have gone perfectly.

That wasn't what the experts said, of course. I

kept hearing at youth work seminars that teachers should put kids in charge more often. Student leadership, they called it. The idea was to let kids learn by doing, to let them sink or swim.

I shuddered. What would my group do with more responsibility? Decide to spend the whole morning watching "The Flintstones"? Student leadership might be fine for others, but not for me. I understood the importance of control. I knew the only way to make things turn out right was to do them yourself.

But after hearing for the hundredth time about this learn-by-doing stuff, I started to feel guilty. In three years of teaching my class, I'd never really done a project with the kids — not one whose success was in their hands. According to the experts I was out of touch, behind the times, inadequate. That wouldn't do.

I decided to try a project, something small. Something like the assignment I'd just finished at work — an original rap song about products, performed on video for salespeople. Our class could study a book of the Bible and create a rap song about it. Maybe we could even perform the rap in church on a Sunday night — if it met my quality standards, of course.

I picked the Bible book — James, a short one and

my favorite. I brought the video of my sales rap and showed it to the class.

The kids watched the monitor silently as the tape played. Then they looked at each other.

"You want us to do *that?*" Adam asked, as if I were requesting that he cut his own throat.

"*I'm* not doing that!" Matt vowed.

I frowned. How was I supposed to give them more responsibility when they didn't want it? But then Joel, thoughtful Joel, said, "That was pretty good." Maybe there was hope, I thought.

The following week we started studying James. I taught in the usual way, then read aloud two rap stanzas I'd written as a model for the class' efforts. I asked the kids to write their first verses during the week, then waited.

The following Sunday Joel brought a few lines and read them shyly. The meter was a little out of kilter, but the message was just right. Dan, on the other hand, had forgotten the assignment. Adam and Matt weren't even there.

I sighed. At this rate, it would take years to finish the rap. This wasn't going to work. I should just write the whole thing myself and forget that wild learning-by-doing theory.

But it was too late to back out. I'd told these guys *we* were going to write a rap, so *we* were. Fortunately, I hadn't inquired about performing it in church; that idea could still slide quietly into oblivion.

We kept studying and summarizing, week after week. Sometimes we'd work on the stanzas in class, but mostly the kids would wrestle with them at home and return with the results scribbled on scraps of paper. Joel wrote about temptations, trials, and taming the tongue. Dan penned stanzas on wisdom and prejudice. Adam came up with verses about rich and poor and the brevity of life. Even Matt contributed a few lines. Slowly something resembling a rap was taking shape.

My spirits rose. Maybe this lead balloon was going to fly after all. I was so enthused that I asked Linda — our pastor's wife and worship planner as well as being Dan's mom — whether we might be able to perform the rap some Sunday night.

Great, she said. But wouldn't it be even greater, she asked, to do it on a Sunday morning? During the worship service? With everybody there?

I gulped. Sure, I replied, even as I told myself the woman was insane.

Now I'd committed myself — and the kids. When

I told them we were slated to perform, their eyes grew wide.

"You're kidding," said Adam.

When they saw that I was serious, their eyes glazed over. They looked as if their only remaining choice were between the electric chair and lethal injection.

Except for Matt. "No way," he said flatly. Maybe he'd carry the boom box, but that was it. I decided to accept that — as if I had a choice.

That week I gathered all those little slips of paper and tapped their contents into my computer, resisting the urge to totally rewrite. Instead I gingerly adjusted a bit of meter here, a rhyme there. I filled in a couple of stanzas we hadn't had time for. But the work of Joel and Dan and Adam and even Matt remained.

So far, so good, I thought. But then we started practicing.

We practiced with an accompaniment track called *Plain White Rapper.* The name was painfully appropriate. We were all quite white, some of us more so than others. I winced as rhythms stumbled, as words were mumbled and inflections got stuck in monotone.

It would be so easy to fix, I thought. I'd only have to tell the kids how to say each word, each line, each verse. But no, this project was supposed to be their own, thanks to those know-it-all youth experts. Maybe, through some miracle, it would get better.

It didn't. We kept practicing, but it was clear that some of us would never get the cadence right. My head began to throb before each rehearsal.

One Sunday, two weeks before Armageddon, Matt changed his mind about not participating. He did it by grabbing Adam's script.

"That's *my* part," Adam protested, grabbing it back.

"I want to be in this too," the younger boy announced. Touched that he wanted to join in, I gave him one of my stanzas to read. Maybe there was something to this student leadership idea after all, I thought.

With one week to go, we rehearsed in costumes—jeans, T-shirts, sunglasses, baseball caps. I wore an old wool sport jacket turned inside out. Even as the kids admired its shredded lining, it was obvious that nervousness was bringing them to the brink of breakdowns.

I was already there.

The big morning hit like a cold shower. Putting on my costume, I was surprised by a call from Linda, the pastor's wife. There'd been a scheduling mixup, she said. The college class was supposed to run the service this morning. They had it all planned. Could my class postpone its rap for a couple of weeks?

Speechless, I nearly crushed the telephone receiver in my fist. Didn't she know the kids were desperate to get this over with? Didn't she know *I* was desperate?

We *really* need to do it this morning, I said, trying not to sound too much like a man at the end of his rope. She said she'd try to work us in somewhere.

My blood pressure off the scale, my stomach clenched, I yanked the rest of my outfit on. I wanted to find those youth experts, dip them in honey, and tie them to an anthill. How could I have let them con me into this? Why hadn't I stuck to the surefire way and made this a one-man show? It was one thing to lay an egg in front of the whole church, but when it could have been so easily *prevented. . . .*

186

An hour later, there we were — the five of us, waiting in the hall next to the church platform. Five pairs of lungs breathed quickly, shallowly. Five pairs of eyes darted here and there, at the clock on the wall, at the mirror. Five pairs of sweaty hands fingered sunglasses and baseball caps and the fake dollar bills that were our props.

Suddenly it was time. I strained to hear our entrance cue, the *Plain White Rapper* music coming from the sanctuary speakers, but there was only silence. I opened the door to the platform, seeing a bumper crop of faces, but still heard nothing.

Completely unhinged now, I considered the logic of strangling the volunteer in the sound booth. I could leap up there, wrap my hands around his throat, and still have time to push the button myself. Yes, that was the way to get things done.

Perhaps reading my thoughts, the sound man finally started the tape. Trying to get into the beat, I led the Gang of Four onto the stage.

This was it, the moment we'd been hurtling toward for the last three months.

The first turn at the microphone was mine. I stabbed an index finger at the crowd and declared in a mock-belligerent voice:

Yo, listen, everybody, and you'll find out
What the high school class is all about!
Oh, yeah, we have our fun and games,
But we've also been studyin' the Book of James.
    It's a letter (hunh!), an epistle, you see,
Written 'tween 45 and 62 A.D. . . .

The *hunh* was grunted in unison by the guys behind me, exactly as we'd rehearsed. Pleasantly surprised, I finished my verse about the authorship of the book, then stepped back.

Joel, red-haired and bespectacled, bopped up to the microphone next:

In chapter 1 James talks about tests
When God is the teacher and life does its best
To smother you with trouble, cover you with pests
And get you to subscribe to its tantalizing jests.
James says to persevere, resist the evil force
  'Cause God don't originate this no-fun course
It's the devil's commercial for sinful desires
For he's the one and only tempter and enticer.

Next was Dan, the pastor's son. He was the only one of us who knew how to do those rap moves

that made you look like you were hugging
yourself:

> *So you say you need wisdom, yeah, I mean*
>   *smarts,*
> *Well, listen up y'all to this here part.*
> *Look on up to God when you're in a real bind*
> *And soon enough the answers you will find.*
> *But there's one condition to this revolution:*
> *You must believe, not doubt God's solution.*
> *'Cause those who doubt are messed in the*
>   *head*
> *And instead of answers, they get nothing*
>   *instead.*

Adam followed, tall and blond and peering down
at his script:

> *Now, moving on to verses 9-11,*
> *James writes about men gettin' to heaven.*
> *Do not worry whether you're rich or poor,*
> *For you can't buy your way through the pearly*
>   *door.*
> *'Cause riches mean nothing to the Lord, you see,*
> *Like a flower, your money will lose its beauty.*

189

And then there was Matt, throwing himself into the performance he'd shunned until the eleventh hour:

> *James says to listen up, put your roots in the Word*
> *And put into action what you've just heard.*
> *Be a doer of the Word, not just a hearer;*
> *Don't be like a man who looks in the mirror*
> *And sees that his nose is out of place,*
> *But when he goes away, he forgets his own face.*
> *Instead, look hard at the perfect law*
> *And remember what you see; fix up that flaw!*

There was more, much more, about hypocrisy and helping widows and orphans, faith and works, selfishness and bitterness, resisting the devil and praying for the sick. There were seventeen stanzas in all, and we delivered them perfectly.

Well, not perfectly. There may have been a few minor problems. Some of us were a bit hard to understand. And some of us seemed completely unaware that a tape was being played in the background, a tape which was in some way related to what we were saying on the stage.

190

But none of that was of the slightest consequence. My guys had *done* it. My brilliant, exasperating, irreplaceable foursome had studied some of the most pointed passages in God's Word. They'd let the truth percolate, thought about how it might apply to them, and come up with their own original way of expressing it.

And now they were up here, full of fear and energy, rapping their hammering hearts out in front of the whole church. I listened, and a wave of pride swept over me, turning to humility by the time I thought about it.

Stepping to the microphone, I belted out the final stanza:

In closing, whether you're adult or youth,
Please bring back the brothers who wander
*   from the truth.*
And that wraps up our rap on James,
So whether or not you remember our names,
Please keep in mind what the Word is for;
When church is over, let's take it out the door!

We all shouted the word *door* together, poking our fingers toward the sanctuary exit. A moment later applause exploded from one wall to the other, and lingered loudly as we made our way off the platform and back into the hall.

Breathless, I turned to look into the faces of Joel and Dan and Adam and Matt. There I saw the kind of light that comes only when you've struck the match yourself.

"That was awesome!" whispered one.

"Let's do it again!" hissed another.

"Let's take it on the road!" said a third.

We took off our caps and sunglasses and went downstairs, then back up to the sanctuary for the rest of the service.

I sat in a pew, my jacket turned right-side-out again. I had a terrible time paying attention to the sermon.

But then maybe I'd already learned enough for one day.

Devotions

FOR THE FIRST THIRTY-SIX YEARS OF MY LIFE, there was nothing I'd rather do than have daily devotions.

Except perhaps to be chained to the caboose of a freight train and dragged facedown over railroad ties from San Francisco to Boston at speeds of up to fifty miles per hour.

Devotions and I just didn't get along.

You might think that growing up in a preacher's house, surrounded by shelves of devotional classics by Oswald Chambers and Hannah Hurnard and Watchman Nee, I'd have acquired a taste for the spiritual disciplines. You might guess that after having all those *Little Visits with God* read to me and my brothers after supper, I'd have developed the "quiet time" habit myself. You might assume that coming from a background in which there was no such thing as less-than-daily devotions, I'd be such a faithful fan of personal Bible reading and prayer that you could set your watch by me.

You would be wrong.

I always had trouble with devotions. Even when I pretended not to.

When I was eleven, for example, I posed briefly as an expert on the devotional life. The opportunity came when I saw a blurb in my Sunday School paper: "How Do You Study the Bible?" We were supposed to send in our successful "quiet time" methods, with $5 offered for each gem printed. Eager for fame and fortune, I found pen and paper and went to work. I'd never been any better at Bible study than most eleven-year-olds were, but I'd recently read a couple of New Testament chapters on my own. So I wrote down an idea I'd used and sent it in.

Sure enough, my handy hint appeared in the paper a year later: "The night before I read, I ask the Holy Spirit to speak to me through God's Word and show me how to live a good Christian life." I got my $5, and was excited to see my name in type, right under the comic strip on page four.

There was only one problem. I'd used my fool-proof formula for about two days after sending it in—then quit. Seeing my words in print a year later reminded me that I'd hardly opened my Bible since. Wondering whether I should return the $5, I put the paper away, feeling like the grimiest of hypocrites.

It was a harbinger of things to come.

For decades after that, two events were inevitable each New Year's Eve: the countdown in Times Square, and my resolution to really, now *really* this time, have daily devotions. And every year one thing was sure by February 1: I would falter and fail.

Soon the very sight of an unopened Bible left me feeling guilty. The guiltier I felt, the more impossible it seemed that I would ever join all those Christians who waved down at me from the heights of devotional bliss.

I couldn't figure out how they'd made it up there. After all, devotions were so *hard*.

For one thing, Scripture seemed to have been designed to keep people from reading it. Genesis and Exodus led to Leviticus; there was no way around it. Every time I'd finish the plagues and murders of the first two books, I'd immediately fall into the tar pits of the third — where I'd try to make my slow and gummy escape, always collapsing and sinking in defeat. Matthew was almost as cruel, forcing me to hurdle a mile of genealogies before I could even get to the New Testament starting line.

I tried switching to devotional booklets, hoping spoonfuls of anecdotes would help the medicine go down. But if the little readings were interesting, I read them all at once — as one might gorge on a whole box of chocolates at a sitting. Most of the booklets weren't so tempting, however, and I didn't read them at all.

As for prayer, the human body seemed designed to shut down at the first sign of it. Trying to pray at bedtime, I fell asleep. Trying it first thing in the morning, I did likewise. My quiet times were quiet indeed — unless I snored.

It didn't even help to hear those inspirational stories, the ones about spiritual giants who seemed to spend half their time having devotions. I couldn't get up at 4 A.M. like A.W. Tozer. I couldn't wash dishes all day like Brother Lawrence, thinking spiritual thoughts amid the suds in the monastery kitchen. I couldn't be like Martin Luther, who said that when facing a hectic day, he spent even more hours of it in prayer than usual. Unlike Luther, I had a lot more to do than sing a few Gregorian chants and nail a list of gripes to the church door. I was *busy.*

I tried changing my expectations from *daily* devotions to *regular* devotions. That worked for a while, but eventually my definition of *regular* stretched from every three days to weekly to monthly to quarterly. Faced with the specter of an annual quiet time, I threw in the towel altogether.

The guilt remained. I still squirmed when older saints stood up during testimony time at church and said, "I'd like to share a passage I was reading in my quiet time this morning. . . . "

But in time the guilt dried up like varnish, and a fine sheen of cynicism was left behind. Now when a saint would stand in church to read a freshly unearthed verse, I would think, *What a weirdo.*

I knew by now that I wasn't the only one who didn't have devotions. I'd seen surveys revealing that plenty of Christians had quiet times less often than they cleaned their ovens. It was comforting, that knowledge. I could go devotionless for the rest of my life and not be a shocking statistic.

And I might have done just that, if not for what happened one hot day in July.

I'd just returned from a convention of Christian bookstore dealers, where my job as an editor was to walk up and down the booth-lined aisles, reconnoitering the competition from other publishers. I'd hiked up and down those aisles for three long days, past endless rows of books and bumper stickers, tapes and key chains, plaques and Scripture sponges.

The more I'd seen, the more I'd been bothered by the gimmicks and the hype. I'd used both in my work too and seeing it all so stark and huge in the convention center left me ashamed. If some of these exhibitors were moneychangers in the temple, so was I.

I'd left the convention wanting to apologize to God, to acknowledge that I'd gotten my place in the universe mixed up with His. Not until I got home, sitting in an empty house in the middle of the afternoon, did I feel I could do it properly.

I sat on the couch and bowed my head. But for some reason I couldn't pray.

My position was wrong, I thought. I'd been thinking of myself more highly than I should, and now I needed to be lower.

I kneeled. I couldn't recall the last time I'd done that, but I tried it now. It didn't feel right, either. I needed to be lower still.

The only other posture I could think of was bowing down like Muslims did when they faced Mecca. *Too strange,* I thought. I never prayed that way. I couldn't.

Yet a moment later I found myself on the floor, down on my face, my forehead to the carpet. Finally it felt right. God was up there; I was down here. *Way* down here.

I started to pray silently, but stopped. It didn't seem to be a time to talk, but to listen. I waited for a long time, still bent to the carpet, the blood pulsing in my ears. After a while my mind cleared, and a verse I'd known for years whispered from my memory:

Be still and know that I am God.

Yes, I was trying to do that. I was trying to repent, to show how far I was below—

Be still and know that I am God.

I kept my face on the floor, eyes closed, and was silent.

Be still and know that I am God.

I sighed. It was so simple, that verse. If only knowing God could be that uncomplicated. If only it weren't a matter of devotions, of a stern system of readings and prayers, a long march of ancient laws and sleepy inner monologues to slog through, rain or shine. If only knowing God weren't something you had to force yourself to do, like going to job interviews and getting your teeth drilled.

Be still and know that I am God.

It sounded like such a great idea — just being quiet and being one of God's creations, with Him infinitely above me and inviting me to get to know Him here below. It sounded almost . . . relaxing.

Bowed down to the floor that afternoon, I suddenly wanted to know the God who would invite me to do such a thing. I longed to meet the One who could be satisfied with silence, the One whose yoke was easier than reading Leviticus at 4 A.M. and whose burden was lighter than praying daily for all the missionaries by name and nation.

I just wanted to be still and know God.

I wanted it so much that the next morning I got up half an hour early and bowed down on the floor again. And the next morning, and the next. I didn't even bring a Bible with me at first. I just cleared my mind and then thought about that verse.

Be still and know that I am God.

Soon I found myself wanting to worship this God who was so high above me. I would talk to Him a little, or think about a hymn. But mostly I was still.

Then I brought a Bible, reading about this God who told the psalmist and Job and Peter and so many others to be quiet, and then I would be quiet too.

A month of mornings became two, then three. Six months passed, and a year. Before I knew it, I'd been meeting with God on the living room carpet nearly every day for a year and a half. Somewhere in there was New Year's Eve — the first I'd ever spent resolving to *continue* with prayer and Bible reading.

But it was no achievement.

It was eating because I was hungry.

It was forgetting the rules and making it up as I went along.

It was Martha, tired of slaving over a hot stove, finally taking the hint and joining Mary at Jesus' feet, just to listen.

It was one of the easiest things I'd ever done.

* * * *

My morning schedule has changed since then — and my back doesn't seem to bend as nimbly as it used to. I've shifted hours and postures, and yes, I've gone for long periods without those times of quiet and worship and reflection.

But the gaps don't make me give up anymore. They make me tired. And hungry.

I may still have a hard time with devotions.

But now I know a great place to rest and have a bite to eat.

The Brother-in-Law

AN AMAZING NUMBER OF PEOPLE seem to
have brothers-in-law who cause problems. You
know the type: deadbeats who keep borrowing
money and never pay it back, freeloaders who stay
at your house and never leave, small-time crooks
who keep having to be bailed out of jail at 2 in the
morning. Terms like ne*'er-do-well* and *black sheep*
and *lazy bum* must have been invented in order to
describe these unsightly branches on the family
tree.

I have a problem brother-in-law too. His name is
John Morton.

To understand John, I guess you'd have to look
first at his childhood. Unfortunately, his childhood
doesn't provide any clues to why he turned out the

way he did. My wife tells me her brother was a perfectly normal boy when he was growing up. Like
any self-respecting older sibling, he was always
putting things in her hair — sand, diaper rash oint-
ment, you name it. He liked to ride around in the
back of a truck with his pals too, squirting pedestrians and bicyclists with a fire extinguisher. He was
just a red-blooded American kid.

Somewhere in there he became a Christian. He
stopped smearing and squirting things on people.
He got interested in their souls instead, and tried
his hand at evangelism. Soon he was what used to
be called "on fire for the Lord," and even enrolled
in seminary to prepare for the ministry.

That was all fine, of course. But one day a man
named Jim Wallis, an editor from a magazine called
Sojourners, came to John's seminary and spoke.
Wallis talked about God's concern for the op-
pressed, and how the church needed to be more
involved in seeing that economic justice was done.

John was never the same after that.

He started getting in trouble at the church
where he'd been volunteering. The church leaders
didn't like him talking to their young people about
things like social justice.

He got rid of his possessions and wore jeans and old shirts all the time. He moved to another seminary, then to a commune in downtown Denver — sharing the little he had with those who had even less. Next he settled in Five Points, a neighborhood plagued by poverty and crime, where he lived in a basement room — not much more than a cell with a bed and a stack of books by philosophers like Jacques Ellul and Søren Kierkegaard.

It didn't take much to support that lifestyle, so John got by with jobs nobody else wanted — substitute teaching in the inner city, working the night shift as an aide in a mental hospital. The rest of the time he roamed the streets, looking for poor people he could help — except when he was sitting in rundown coffee shops, reading his Bible and writing in his journal.

Eventually it wasn't enough for John to walk the most treacherous streets of Denver. He decided to travel the world, going wherever he thought God wanted him to go. To the former Yugoslavia, wracked by civil war. To inner-city Washington, D.C. To France, where he helped care for disabled people in a Christian community called *L'Arche* — The Ark.

I prayed for John, of course, when he headed for the world's dangerous and needy places. But I also breathed a little easier when he wasn't around. That's because being with John sometimes made me . . . uncomfortable.

A few years ago, for instance, I ran into John at a family gathering in Arizona. I was tired and tense from months of meeting deadlines at work. John looked at me in that concerned but tranquil way of his and asked, "Why do you have to work so much?"

I frowned. What was *that* supposed to mean? Was he suggesting I didn't need that mortgage, those certificates of deposit, that pension plan? He'd never understand the responsibilities of *real* life, I thought.

Irritated, I pulled a dollar bill from my wallet and waved it in front of him. "For this!" I said. *"This* is why I have to work so much!"

"I hear what you're saying," John replied gently. That's all he said, but for some reason the word *mammon* kept running through my mind.

Then there was the time John stayed for a couple of days at our house, on his way back from living in Poland for a year. He'd been teaching English and sharing his faith there.

The first evening of his visit went well enough, as he told us funny stories about things like standing in a Polish food line and having to flap his arms and cluck like a chicken because he didn't know the word for *egg*. But the second night I made the mistake of taking him to one of *our* supermarkets.

Trying to make conversation on the way, I asked what he'd learned in Poland.

"That it's possible to endure poverty with great dignity," he said.

Oh, great, I thought. What would he think of our giant grocery-pharmacy-variety-liquor store with its fax machine and video lottery game?

At the store we wound our way past the bananas and kiwi fruit, the frozen cheesecakes and gummy worms, the pre-sliced, pull-tab convenience foods — things John couldn't have gotten in Poland no matter how long he'd stood in line. At last we reached the aisle where I could get a box of granola bars for John's train ride home to Denver.

"What kind would you like?" I asked.

He stared at the shelf. There must have been a dozen different types — large and small, chewy and crunchy, with and without peanut butter and cinnamon and honey and raisins and chocolate.

"Oh," he sighed, "it really doesn't matter."

He said no more, but he'd said it all. Having the world's greatest choice of granola bars just didn't seem to matter when John was around. Neither did a lot of other things I spent time and energy on.

Finally there was the last time I saw John, just a few weeks ago. This time he'd been in Guatemala — working in an orphanage. He was going back to Poland, where he would try again to endure poverty with great dignity.

He stayed at our house for a couple of days before his plane left. While he stayed, he told us how concerned he was about the Guatemalan orphans, how scared he'd felt when he'd been stopped at night by the military, how he'd nearly drowned swimming off the coast — and how, when he'd thought he was about to die, he'd seen the faces of people who meant the most to him.

Just before he had to leave our house, John sat on the living room sofa and looked tired. He'd lost the wanderlust of his youth, he said, but still traveled because he believed God wanted him to.

"But I'm not special," he said. "If people compared themselves carefully to me, they'd discover more similarities than they imagine. I face the same temptations they do. I'm still figuring out what it means to be a Christian.''

He quoted one of those philosophers, Søren Kierkegaard: '''Tis a poor soldier who does not desire to be a general.'' That was John's hope: to keep improving as a soldier in the kingdom.

"So what's your current rank?" I asked.

"Latrine boy," he said.

Then it was time for him to go, to catch his plane to Poland. Unable to drive John to the airport that day, we'd called one of those limo services to pick him up.

As we heard the car pull into the driveway, John gathered up his earthly possessions — a single duffel bag of clothes, a backpack full of books, a Bible so well-worn there was no cover left, and his journal.

He walked out to the driveway, where idled the longest stretch limousine I'd ever seen — at least thirty feet long, white, the kind of novelty car a whole wedding party could ride in while drinking champagne from the bar and watching TV. *Enchanted,* said a sign in its window.

The driver held the door open, and John slid

into the gray luxury interior. He sat there wearing his jeans and T-shirt, looking more out of place than I'd ever thought anyone could look.

He didn't say anything, naturally. He didn't have to.

The car was so long it could barely manuever back onto the street without hitting the neighbors' mailboxes. I waved, and John was gone.

Gone with his handful of possessions, his compassion for people he hadn't yet met, his willingness to sacrifice his life, his determination to do the will of his Father.

He reminds me of Somebody, John does.

Someone quite unlike myself.

And that, of course, is the problem.

Little Things

APPARENTLY I DID SOMETHING IMPORTANT
the year I was a junior in high school. I just can't
remember what it was.

Whatever it was, I must have done it in front of
Wayne. He went to my school, where the only class
we had in common was P.E. I was barely conscious
of the fact that he sat a few benches away in the
locker room, changing into gym shorts with the
rest of us. I don't remember speaking to him.

About halfway through the year I noticed that
Wayne had started coming to our church youth
group. I hadn't brought him, and didn't know who
had.

One night Wayne stood up to give his testimony.
He'd just become a Christian, and wanted to ex-

plain why. "I saw people like John at school," he said. "There was something different in their lives, and I wanted what they had."

Shocked, I looked around the room to see whether there were any other Johns in the group. There weren't. He was talking about me.

I had goose bumps. God had used *me* to help bring somebody to Jesus.

But *Wayne?*

What had he seen me do? Refuse to listen to one of those notorious locker-room jokes? Discourage someone from snapping another guy with a wet towel? Carry a Bible to campus one day? Ask the blessing over my lunch in the cafeteria?

It didn't seem proper to ask Wayne what I'd done, so I never did. To this day, I have no idea what it was.

Except that it must have been a little thing — so little I didn't even know I'd done it.

* * * *

Apparently we did something important, Liz and I, the day we had Samuel over for dinner. For a long time, though, we didn't know what it was.

It had made us nervous, the idea of having Samuel over. He was from Nigeria, and we didn't know what Nigerians liked to eat or how they liked to eat it. We also didn't know what they liked to do before or after they ate.

We did know, though, that Samuel loved Jesus. In our Bible study group he was always speaking urgently, with that softly musical accent, about the need to love and serve Christ with all our hearts. He knew a lot about that subject, having sacrificed much to study in the U.S. so that someday he could return to Africa as a pastor. He'd even had to leave his wife and children behind for the duration. Just when we'd start feeling sorry for him, however, he'd break into a gentle grin. "Praise da Lord," he would say.

As the day of our dinner approached, Liz and I dithered over what to serve our special guest. Everything we thought of seemed too American. Finally we gave up, settling on the simplest thing we could think of — chicken cooked on the backyard grill. It wasn't much, but it would have to do.

Somehow we made it through that dinner. Samuel was earnest and polite as always. We felt privileged to have him in our home.

But an odd thing happened after that. Nearly every time we saw him, Samuel thanked us profusely for having him over, recalling the chicken we'd had and praising it to the skies. We couldn't understand why he was so enthused about such a basic meal.

Until a few years later, when I met a woman who'd served as a missionary to Uganda. When I told her about Samuel and the chicken, she nodded as if the explanation were obvious. "In many villages in Africa," she said, "when you want to show special honor to a guest, you kill a chicken and cook it for dinner." Roasting it, she said. Sort of like on a barbecue grill.

It had been so easy, serving chicken on a Sunday afternoon. But to Samuel it was a banquet, a ticker-tape parade of welcome.

It was such a little thing — so little we didn't know how much it meant.

*   *   *   *

Apparently I did something important that Thanksgiving Day at church. But it wasn't what I'd thought it would be.

I'd spent the whole afternoon in the church basement, helping with our annual Thanksgiving

Day outreach dinner—hauling steaming vats of turkey and potatoes and green beans until my arms ached, serving platefuls to the multitudes who'd come from the neighborhood, from nursing homes, from other congregations. I'd pitched in with the evangelistic program down the hall too, starting things off with a high-energy skit.

I hadn't had time to eat a bite of Thanksgiving dinner myself. When the program ended I was tired and hungry—but pleased with myself for delivering such an outstanding afternoon of Christian service. Watching our guests walk, shuffle, and wheel back to the dining hall, I heard my stomach growl and hoped a few bites of turkey and dressing were left for me.

Wanting to unplug an adding machine we'd used during the skit, I followed the path of the extension cord—then halted. Between me and the electrical outlet was an elderly woman slumped in a wheelchair, dozing. If I woke her up, she might want to talk—maybe even tell me her life story. I'd never get out of here, and never get my Thanksgiving dinner.

Tiptoeing toward the plug, I held my breath. But the old lady awoke, and I was trapped.

Sighing, I stepped back and looked at her. She could barely hold her head up, it seemed. A grimace crossed her yellowish, wrinkled face as if she were in pain.

"Is there . . . something I can get you?" I asked, not knowing what else to say.

Slowly her bleary eyes found me. Her dry lips parted and I heard a hoarse whisper.

"Just . . . a cup . . . of cold water," she said.

As I realized where I'd heard that phrase before, a chill sped down my spine. Those were the words of Jesus:

"And if anyone gives even a cup of cold water to one of these little ones because he is My disciple, I tell you the truth, he will certainly not lose his reward" (Matt. 10:42).

Suddenly I wasn't hungry anymore.

I fetched the water in a styrofoam cup and placed it in the lady's shaking hands. She could barely get it to her lips without spilling it, but managed to work on it a tiny sip at a time.

Between sips she would complain of feeling sick, then look as if she were about to doze again. But then she would perk up and tell me something that had happened to her once, a shred of the past with no year attached, whether from girlhood or adulthood she didn't seem to know.

I just listened and asked an occasional question and watched that cup, thinking about the words of Jesus and how I'd almost missed them. Three minutes stretched to half an hour, then longer.

I don't think I ever did eat dinner that Thanksgiving Day. But for some reason it was the most meaningful Thanksgiving I'd ever had.

It was such a little thing, giving someone a cup of water — so little I almost didn't do it at all.

* * * *

God seems interested in little things. A widow's coin. The washing of a foot. The surrender of a small boy's loaves and fish.

He makes much of little things — as much as He wants to.

He may call us to move mountains once in a while, but the rest of the time He has plenty of molehills to be relocated. He probably wants more encouraging notes sent than books written, more sandwiches shared than sermons preached, more Band-Aids applied than edifices built.

That's good news for those of us who have only

little things to work with.

Like a cup of water.

Or a chicken.

Or a word or deed so tiny it can't even be remembered — except by the recipient, who may never, ever forget.

Katherine

IT IS JUST BEFORE THE STROKE OF MIDNIGHT, March 10, 1989. I am about to pull my sweater off and go to bed, but something more important happens.

"I think my water broke," says my wife Liz, lifting her head from her pillow.

I stand up straight, suddenly shot full of adrenaline.

We are going to have a baby.

After fourteen years of marriage, after six long years of trying, after tests and surgery and prescriptions, after the pain of three early miscarriages, we are finally going to have a baby.

We've been so careful not to get our hopes too high, but now the time has come. The pregnancy has gone so well, and we are just three weeks from the official due date. We've taken care of everything — nursery, cradle, diaper service, sleepers, toys.

So this is what it feels like, I think, quickly packing a few last-minute items into Liz's overnight bag. *The beginning of a new life.*

But I do not know what it feels like, not yet.

We take our places in a homelike birthing room at Central DuPage Hospital in Winfield, Illinois. Contractions are beginning. Liz starts to use the breathing exercises we've practiced in prenatal class. The nurses smile reassuringly.

But then everything changes.

Something goes wrong. The nurses' eyes register panic as they stare at the fetal monitor's readout. My heartbeat quickens as our unborn baby's heartbeat drops. The call goes out for a doctor.

I hold Liz's hand as a tall man in a white coat rushes in. Suddenly Liz is on her hands and knees, and someone is holding a clipboard in front of me. There are forms there, papers for me to sign.

"Emergency C-section," someone says.

The pen quivers in my hand. I remember the discussion of cesarean sections in the prenatal class just a couple of nights ago. All of us thought it would happen to somebody else.

The papers are taken away, my signature wobbly. Liz is wheeled from the room, from the grip of my hand. Drops of bright red blood trail the stainless steel cart. I follow it, but it pushes through doors beyond which I am forbidden.

I lean against the wall, my eyes closed. I pray silently.

"Are you all right?" asks a young nurse.

"I'm fine," I say, purely out of habit.

She shows me to a seat at the nurses' station and asks me to wait. She gives me a can of Sprite, then leaves. The can is cold in my hand. I feel cold all over.

For a long time no one comes to tell me anything. I know that the longer I hear nothing, the worse the news will be.

Just after 4:30 A.M. the young nurse walks up. "You have a little girl," she says. She sounds neither cheery nor sad, almost statistical. She asks what my newborn's name is, and pulls out a clipboard.

For several seconds I pause, my mind fighting the numbness, and then I remember.

"Katherine. Katherine Ann Duckworth." I spell it.

I seem unable to ask more than a couple of the questions that are screaming to get out, and the nurse seems reluctant to answer them. All I learn is that Liz is OK, that our baby is "very small," that "the doctor is working with her." The nurse leaves, and I sit, growing colder, the numbness overtaking me.

Eventually I am handed a green outfit, the kind worn in operating rooms, with plastic cap and shoe covers. I am to put it on so that I can see my little girl. I put it on in the birthing room, then sit in a chair. I gaze into the hall, up at the lights.

"Though He slay me, yet will I trust Him."

The verse from Job floats into my head. I am surprised that I agree with the words — as much as I am able, as much as the cold and numbness and confusion will let me. I turn the verse into a prayer:

Though You slay me, yet will I trust You.

Even as I pray, I wonder what is yet to come.

After more waiting, two doctors come in. The tall one is the stranger who performed the emergency delivery. The short one is an obstetrician from our clinic. They shake hands with me.

The short one explains that he has seen Katherine. Our baby weighs just three pounds, one ounce. Her length is thirteen and one-half inches. She did not start breathing on her own at birth; they had to force air into her lungs with a rubber bag. Now something called a ventilator is helping her to breathe in the intensive care nursery.

"I'm almost certain she has a trisome," the doctor says. An extra chromosome. A genetic anomaly. A birth defect.

And then he breaks the news: Our baby's condition will probably take her life within a week. Perhaps a month. Maybe a year.

"Even if that's not what she has, that little girl has a rough time ahead of her," he says. A test will tell us what the problem is. The results won't come back for three days.

I thank the doctors when they leave. Then I sit down, staring blankly. Soon I am shivering uncontrollably.

The nurse discovers me like this and brings me a blanket. It has been preheated somehow. I huddle in it until she comes to get me, to take me to the intensive care nursery.

It is time to meet Katherine.

I step into the high-tech nursery as a diver steps into an airlock, from one world to another. Everything is clean and bright. The monitors and pumps and IV stands tower over the clear plastic cradles. There are mechanical clicks and beeps and hisses, but no crying.

A neonatologist, also dressed in green, starts explaining something to me. She is from the Middle East, and I have a hard time picking up everything she says. I learn that Katherine is to be taken to Loyola University Medical Center near Chicago. Her condition is too precarious, even for this roomful of futuristic equipment.

I am led to one of the little beds. The nurse pulls up a stool for me, and I sit. I am afraid to look, but I do, and here is the smallest baby I have ever seen. Her legs, no thicker than my thumb, are flailing erratically. Her face is squinched up, crying, but there is no sound. There are tubes in her mouth and nose, secured with tape.

My fingers move to stroke the tiny, reddened feet that kick and tremble. Her skin is so thin, so fragile. "It's OK," I keep saying, "It's OK," as if the words could make things right. She is having seizures, I am told, as she has had since birth.

224

I keep stroking anyway, until I notice that a few of the toes on each foot are fused together. For the briefest moment I pull my hand away, and then, ashamed, resume the stroking and the soothing words.

The nurse at my elbow hands me tissues from a box. I had not noticed my own tears.

Another nurse snaps a Polaroid picture of Katherine and hands it to me. It is not a very good picture, I think. But then I realize we may never get another, and I hold it tightly.

When I leave the nursery ten minutes later, I wonder whether I have seen Katherine for the last time.

Liz is waiting in her room, half dozing. She is no longer in the maternity ward, subject to the sight of happy parents and healthy infants. She has been moved to another floor, to a private room, to grieve.

When she seems lucid I try to explain what has happened. Through a morphine haze she listens, her expression suspended between sorrow and sleep. "All they would tell me . . . was that the doctor would be talking to me," she manages. "I knew something was wrong."

I show her the photograph, the one that shows a tiny baby taped and tubed and wired. She half sighs, half cries, and it is clear that the only thing in the world she wants is to hold her child.

Before long the neonatologist from Loyola arrives. He is Jonathan Muraskas, a balding man with a gentle voice, kind eyes, infinite patience. He wheels into the room a clear plastic incubator, a sort of traveling intensive care unit. Inside is Katherine, her seizures now calmed by barbiturates. She looks smaller than ever. Dr. Muraskas explains where our baby will be. I can come and visit her anytime; after Liz is released from Central DuPage, she can visit too. And we can call the neonatal intensive care unit twenty-four hours a day to find out how Katherine is doing.

He explains the test that will take three days to analyze. Do we have any questions? We can't think of any, only because we can't think of anything at all. Dr. Muraskas understands, and says that we can call him anytime too.

And then he goes, and Katherine is wheeled away to an ambulance. Liz strains to lift her head, to catch a glimpse, and I see the anguish written on her pale and weary face.

Then it is quiet. Reluctantly I make one phone call after another, to parents, to friends. I struggle to control my voice, and those I call struggle to find theirs.

Liz sleeps, wakes, sleeps again. When we find the energy, we hug and cry. Our pastor and his wife visit. Our friends Stan and Pam and Paul come by. No one knows what to say, but no one has to.

Late that night, Saturday night, I find my way out of the hospital and to my car. I go home, finally pull off my sweater, and fall into bed. I have been up for forty-one hours. Once more the tears come, and then I fall asleep.

*   *   *   *

It is the next morning, Sunday.

Churches in Illinois, Oregon, and Colorado are already praying for Katherine and for us. Our friends Chris and Julie Grant offer to take me to Loyola for my first visit, and I am grateful. Julie is a nurse, and will be able to explain things as we go along.

The neonatal intensive care unit at Loyola is several times the size of the one at Central DuPage. Chris and Julie and I must check in at a window,

227

then wash at big basins, rubbing up to our elbows with orange-yellow antiseptic before we can be admitted.

We enter a vast room filled with row after row of tiny beds, each set into its own portable framework of monitors, heat lamps, pumps, alarms, and digital readouts. There are at least two dozen beds, and nearly that many rocking chairs.

A nurse shows us to Katherine's station. I sit in a rocker, and the nurse prepares to let me hold Katherine for the first time. The ventilator tube is removed just long enough to make the transition from bed to lap, but even in those twenty seconds or so I watch in horror as Katherine's skin turns bluish-gray. We are going to lose her now, I think. Liz will not get to see her.

But when the tube is replaced, her color improves. The numbers on the blood oxygen monitor increase. Relieved, I stare at the seemingly weightless bundle in my arms.

She is impossibly tiny, almost lost in the quilted pillow that supports her. Her head is no larger than an orange; each hand is smaller than the safety pin that holds her IV bandage to her pillow. Her eyes are shut as usual, her hands perpetually clenched.

Despite the tubes for breathing and suction, despite the white and silver electrode patches, I can see how beautiful she is. The extra chromosome, if there is one, seems to have done little external damage. She has fine, brown hair, a button nose. On the rare occasions that she opens her eyes, they are black and shining as obsidian.

I kiss her forehead and feel the slightest hint of fuzz, smell the sweetness, and tell myself that I must never forget the softness of her skin against my lips.

I whisper her name in her ear over and over. I tell her about her mommy, about her grandparents, her aunts and uncles and cousins. I try to include them all, knowing it may be my last chance.

Julie Grant takes pictures. I take some too after Katherine is returned to bed. Julie has brought a bunny toy, and we prop that in a corner of the crib.

It is time to meet with Dr. Muraskas. We do so in an office, the Grants and I. The doctor sketches diagrams on a memo pad to explain the problems in Katherine's body that have been discovered by X-ray and other means. She cannot eat or drink, since her esophagus does not reach her stomach. She is microcephalic — having a small head and correspondingly small brain, meaning that she will be profoundly retarded if she survives. But survival is unlikely, because the seemingly end-less list of problems includes major heart defects.

If she has Trisomy 18, as the doctor suspects, it is only a matter of time. This is "a condition incom-patible with life," as a book on his shelf puts it. Only 1 in 2,400 live births involves this syndrome; most victims live only a few hours, days, or weeks. A few go home with parents for constant care until another illness — pneumonia, for example — proves too much for them. A miniscule minority live until their teenage years.

I thank the doctor, and the Grants, who take our pictures to a one-hour developer. The prints will find their way to the bulletin board in Liz's hospital room, over the floral arrangements that are multi-plying there. Visitors will smile and sigh over the baby in the photographs, trying gallantly to look beyond the tubes and wires.

My Monday is a marathon of shuttling between hospitals. At Central DuPage I see Liz's parents who have just driven here from Colorado, trying to support us despite the grief that weighs them down. At Loyola I meet Kim, the Christian social worker who offers help as well.

That night Liz is allowed a brief escape from Central DuPage. Entering Loyola in a wheelchair, still wearing a hospital gown, she holds her baby for the first time and smiles through her tears.

On Tuesday the test results come back: Trisomy 18. No one is surprised. Now the question is not what, but when.

Tuesday afternoon we almost lose her. The doctor on duty at Loyola calls us at Central DuPage, reporting that Katherine has had a bad spell but rallied. Little by little, her heart is beginning to fail. He wants to know: If her heart stops again, do we want CPR performed on her?

Friends are milling around the room, chatting, as I listen to this stranger ask his life-or-death question. I ask the doctor whether resuscitating Katherine would cause her pain. It could, he says. Feeling she has suffered enough, we tell the doctor that if our baby slips away, not to use such measures to bring her back.

It could happen any time now, we realize. Subconsciously we begin to wait for the phone to ring again, this time with a final message.

I go home for a while, as I have been doing at
night and some mealtimes, feeling alien in my own
house. I find myself doing what I never do, flipping
my Bible open just to see where it lands, hoping it
will land in a place that means something right
now.

It opens to 2 Corinthians 4:7-9, 12, 16-18:

*"But we have this treasure in jars of clay to
show that this all-surpassing power is from God
and not from us. We are hard pressed on every
side, but not crushed; perplexed, but not in despair; persecuted, but not abandoned; struck
down, but not destroyed. . . . So then, death is at
work in us, but life is at work in you. . . . Therefore we do not lose heart. Though outwardly
we are wasting away, yet inwardly we are being
renewed day by day. For our light and momen-
tary troubles are achieving for us an eternal glory
that far outweighs them all. So we fix our eyes not
on what is seen, but on what is unseen. For what
is seen is temporary, but what is unseen is
eternal."*

Later it opens to Romans 8:22-23, 36-39:

*"We know that the whole creation has been
groaning as in the pains of childbirth right up to
the present time. Not only so, but we ourselves,
who have the firstfruits of the Spirit, groan inwardly as we wait eagerly for our adoption as
sons, the redemption of our bodies. . . . As it is
written: 'For your sake we face death all day
long; we are considered as sheep to be slaugh-
tered.' No, in all these things we are more than
conquerors through Him who loved us. For I am
convinced that neither death nor life, neither angels nor demons, neither the present nor the
future, nor any powers, neither height nor depth,
nor anything else in all creation, will be able to
separate us from the love of God that is in Christ
Jesus our Lord."*

Alone in my empty house I read these words and
groan like all creation. My groan turns to a wail,
and I weep long and hard because of all I am learning about this present world, and all I wish I knew
about the next.

Late Tuesday afternoon Liz is released from the
hospital. We trace and retrace the forty-five-minute
route between our home and Katherine's, spend-

ing as much time with her as we can. We hold her
for hours, watching the numbers on the monitors
climb and plummet. Whenever they dip too low,
alarms sound and a nurse comes running. But
Katherine stays alive.

She stays Wednesday to hear the lullaby I wrote
for her months ago. She stays Thursday to be held
by my parents, who have flown in from Oregon to
see their first grandchild and embrace us tearfully.
She stays for a visit from our pastor, and a sponge
bath and diaper change from Liz and me. She stays
while we carefully snip a lock of her hair and put it
in a little bag as much more than a memento of
babyhood.

But she cannot stay forever. Her circulatory system is failing. It is getting harder and harder to
find a place in her tiny arms and feet to insert
the IV needle. She is suffering, and keeping her on
the breathing apparatus is beginning to seem
cruel.

We meet with Dr. Muraskas. It is decided that
Katherine will be taken off the ventilator at 4 P.M.
on Friday. "Then we'll see what God will do," says
the doctor in his gentle voice.

We go home and begin to make funeral arrange-

ments. We start planning the memorial service
with our pastor and his wife.

*   *   *   *

It is Friday, 4 P.M.

Liz and I ride the elevator up to the neonatal intensive care unit. Our parents are back at our
house, waiting and praying.

There is a room at Loyola in which things like
this happen, a room next to the one where Katherine lives. It is a small, windowless room with light
green walls and two fold-out chairs on which parents can sleep when they are staying the night. It is
to this room that Liz and I go.

We sit on the fold-out chairs and wait. I have
brought a camera. We have learned this week to
take as many pictures as we can.

My heart is in my throat as Katherine is brought
in. Dr. Muraskas has prepared us for the possibility
that she may have only moments left, but to everyone's surprise she is breathing on her own for the
first time.

And for the first time, we see her whole face,
without the tubes or tape. Her tiny mouth is like a
jewel, as silent as always, but pink and perfect.

235

She is unfettered now by electrodes and monitors. There are no fluctuating readouts to stare at in this room, no alarms to dread. There is only an IV stand and a tube connected to her foot, through which she receives nourishment.

She wears the smallest outfit we could find, a newborn-size T-shirt with a rabbit on it. It looks like a tent on her miniature frame; her weight has dipped to two pounds, fourteen ounces.

The doctor and nurses leave. Liz holds her first, on a pink and blue and white crocheted blanket. I try to keep my hands from shaking as I take one picture after another. A few times Katherine opens her eyes, and we say, "Oh, look!" as if we have seen a shooting star or spouting whale, while in reality we have seen something far more special.

I have used up the film. She is still alive.

My heart thunders in my chest as I drop to my knees and pray aloud, knowing that she could be gone by the time I say amen. "Into Your hands we commend her spirit," I pray, the monumental words sticking in my throat.

She is still with us. We take turns holding her and waiting. Every twenty minutes or so the nurse comes in to listen for a pulse. The heart rate keeps dropping.

Late afternoon turns to evening, evening to night. The nurse dims the room lights in case one of us wants to sleep, and it seems that we are more than ever in the valley of the shadow. Katherine's heart rate dives as low as fifteen beats per minute, and we think surely we will lose her now. But she hangs on.

"It's all right," Liz and I whisper to her, much as I had told Katherine when we first met. But now we are saying that it's all right to let go. We tell her that Jesus loves her and is waiting to put His arms around her. I am awed at how close heaven feels; for Katherine the door is right here in this room.

We sing to her again, and this time the song is "Jesus Loves Me," the words taking on new meaning:

Jesus loves me, this I know
For the Bible tells me so
Little ones to Him belong
They are weak, but He is strong . . .

She is not ready to go yet. We keep holding her. A little later we try to sing her another song, a favorite about help in hard times, "Bridge over

Troubled Water.'' But our voices choke on the significance of the last verse:

Sail on, silvergirl,
Sail on by
Your time has come to shine,
All your dreams are on their way.
  See how they shine. . . .

In the middle of the night the nurse asks whether she can pray with us. A devout Catholic, she kneels and murmurs quietly:

Hail, Mary, full of grace,
The Lord is with thee;
Blessed art thou among women. . . .

Her gesture of caring leaves us silent, touched. We are grateful again at 2 or 3 A.M. when she offers to hold Katherine so that we
can go downstairs to stretch our legs and get a drink.

The hallways of the great hospital are nearly deserted. We find a small room lined with vending machines. We are too tired to say much as we eat a hastily chosen snack.

We return to the room, and Liz sleeps. I hold Katherine, determined not to doze. She appears to be straining now, gasping for breath. Her heart rate is down to a mere seven beats per minute. I beg God to take her home.

Finally my watch says it is morning. Saturday morning, one week after Katherine's birth. Around 7:30 I lie down as Liz holds our little girl.

I close my eyes. When I open them it is 8.

"I think she's gone," Liz says quietly, looking down at the peaceful bundle in her lap.

Dazed, I go out to get the nurse. She gets Dr. Muraskas, and they come in. The doctor puts his stethoscope to Katherine's tiny chest. We wait for a long time.

At last he speaks. "She's in heaven," he says simply.

We ask for a few more minutes with her, and are left alone. Liz passes the featherweight body to me, and I hold it to my chest, cradling the precious head under my chin. I touch the softness, the wispy hair, the ebbing warmth I must never forget. I draw a deep breath, and a shuddering sob escapes from somewhere deep inside.

And at that moment, in a place so close yet so far away, on the other side of the door that is this room, a little girl is whole and happy, running and dancing in the Light. There are no tears where she is. No seizures, no defects, no gasping for breath.

I hug what she has left behind. I look through bloodshot eyes across the little room at the brave and beautiful woman who has spent this night as I have, peering into the darkness and sensing the radiant welcome of the Light Himself.

And together, without speaking, we fix our eyes on what is unseen, for that is eternal.

It is why, though we are hard pressed on this bleak March morning, we are not crushed.

And it is why, though our sadness seems unbearable, we are convinced as never before that neither death nor life, nor anything else in all creation, can separate us from the love of God that is in Christ Jesus our Lord.

Nor from our daughter, Katherine.

The Land of the Living

TRYING TO LOOK CALM, I glanced around the clinic waiting room. Most of the patients were pregnant women. A few were older men. We were all thinking about the same thing: the invisible, the threats and promises we couldn't see.

This was the Imaging Department of the clinic, the place where people went to discover through X-ray and ultrasound the hidden secrets of their bodies. For my wife Liz and me, it was a place for hope as well as fear.

Sitting in the chair next to mine, Liz kept shifting uncomfortably and looking at the clock. Her bladder felt ready to burst, she said, from all the water the nurse had given her to drink. It was standard preparation for this kind of ultrasound — the kind that revealed the greatest secret of all, an unborn baby.

A baby. It was hard to believe we were going through this again, especially after Katherine. It had been wrenching enough to wrestle with infertility for six years, and to suffer three early miscarriages. But then we'd lost our first and only child. Katherine had lived just a week, her life stolen by a genetic abnormality.

We knew it could happen again, though genetic testing had shown nothing wrong with our chromosomes. Staring at photos of our squiggly genes, we'd been told by a genetic counselor that the chances of our having another baby with a fatal problem were the same as any other couple's — small.

So what? I'd thought. *The chances were small last time too.* Statistics meant little since I'd carried my daughter's tiny casket to her grave. In such a fallen world, there was no point in giving odds.

Yet we'd tried again. We'd tried because our week with Katherine had opened a new room in our hearts, a child-sized room, and it was empty. We'd tried because we were running out of time; Liz would soon turn thirty-five, when the likelihood of birth defects would be even greater.

We'd tried, and the morning after Thanksgiving, 1989, a little paper strip from Liz's home pregnancy test had turned blue. A few days later the doctor's office had confirmed it: We were expecting again.

But there had been no dramatic embrace, no "That's great, Honey!" We'd been through this too many times before, only to be disappointed. We kept our secret, waiting for the sudden cramps or bleeding that could signal another miscarriage.

Six weeks crawled by, and nothing happened. Finally we told relatives and friends our news. Many began to pray.

They'd prayed before, of course. They'd prayed during Liz's seemingly normal pregnancy with Katherine, and that had gone awry. It was clear that there were no surefire incantations, no words that would force God to give us a healthy baby. There was only waiting, and praying with no guarantees.

I'd been praying every morning, and reading Scripture, clinging to the Psalms as if they were a life raft in a hurricane. One morning I'd come across these verses and moored my battered faith to them:

243

"I believe that I shall see the goodness of the Lord in the land of the living! Wait for the Lord; be strong, and let your heart take courage; yea, wait for the Lord!" (Ps. 27:13-14, RSV)

I knew there was no promise here for me, no prophecy. There was only an echo of my hope, and a reminder of how steady were the hands in which we waited.

And now we were waiting here, at the clinic on a February afternoon, wondering what our first ultrasound would show. All week I'd thought of little else — except the fear that if this child was healthy, Liz might want another. *I can't go through this again,* I thought. If only we could get it over with in one nine-month free-fall, one excruciating, breath-holding hurtle toward the unknown . . .

The nurse called Liz's name.

Minutes later we were in a darkened room. Liz lay on the examining table, her swelling tummy smeared with gel. A technician, a young woman, glided a microphone-shaped sensor back and forth on Liz's abdomen.

I watched blurry shadows on the black-and-white screen. Liz answered questions about her pregnancy, moaned about the water pressure in her belly, and mentioned that she'd been taking a fertility drug before conception.

"You sure did," said the woman, looking at the screen.

Then I saw it—or rather *them.* There were two miniscule shapes fidgeting in the sea of gray.

"It's twins," the technician said.

"What?" Liz cried in disbelief, twisting her neck to see the screen. I felt a goofy smile form on my face. *Two at once,* I thought. It was almost as if God had been preparing me for this, reminding me of the advantage of getting two babies for the price of one gestation.

But my relief was short-lived. At our next visit the doctor informed us that twins were automatically a high-risk pregnancy. There were things that could go wrong with multiples—like prematurity, or one twin failing to thrive. Liz would have to be on bed rest starting in April; a cesarean delivery was planned for July, assuming we made it that far.

I began to pray harder, and to tighten my grip on that verse:

"I believe that I shall see the goodness of the Lord in the land of the living."

One evening, just four months into the pregnancy, Liz began bleeding. *This is it,* I thought, bracing myself for another loss. Liz went to the hospital for tests. The verdict: Everything seemed OK.

We continued the countdown, each week passing as slowly as a geologic age.

There were more ultrasounds, five in all, each preceded by thoughts of disaster and followed by easier breathing. We were transfixed by fuzzy glimpses of Baby A pointing an index finger, of Baby B's miniature jaw making a chewing motion. There were the palpitating hearts, the fragile spines.

But even as we watched we knew there were dangers the ultrasounds could not uncover. All we could do was pray, and wait, and follow doctor's orders.

Liz began her bed rest, spending most of it on the couch. As she read stacks of parenting books, forty pounds attached themselves to the middle of her 5'2" frame.

We felt the babies moving, kicking. We talked to them, sang to them. I decorated the nursery, a different room from the one we'd prepared for Katherine. I assembled the cribs, wiping them meticulously with antiseptic and tightening all the screws, and wondered whether two babies would ever really sleep in them.

As time grew short, Liz went to the hospital weekly for monitoring of the babies' heartbeats and movements. The doctors seemed satisfied, but I was uneasy. Why did one baby move frequently under my hand while the other barely moved at all? There were just too many things that could go wrong, I thought. Too many problems undetectable until the babies had gone from their world into ours.

That transition was scheduled for the morning of July 24. Unless, of course, the babies — boys, we guessed from the ultrasounds — decided to come sooner.

They didn't. In the wee hours of July 24 we drove toward Central DuPage Hospital, where Katherine had been born. Predawn mist rose from fields along the road, mysterious as our future.

After check-in, things happened quickly. We changed into hospital garb, then waited along with other couples as if in the wings of a theater. A few words from the anesthesiologist, and Liz was wheeled into the operating room.

Sent to wait in the hall as she was prepped for surgery, I sat alone on a sofa. The terror of that early morning flooded back, that morning sixteen months before when I'd waited alone on this floor of this hospital during Katherine's emergency delivery. I knew how wrong things could go, how instantly and harshly the world could change.

"I believe that I shall see the goodness of the Lord in the land of the living! Wait for the Lord; be strong, and let your heart take courage."

I fastened my mind to those verses and prayed. I looked up at the clock, then prayed again. I gazed around the waiting area, thinking that this would be the last time I sat on a sofa or looked at a clock before *it* happened. I knew everything would be different in half an hour or so, but I did not know how.

"OK—you can come in now."

It was a nurse, smiling at me.

The operating room was chillier than I'd expected, and larger, and full of people — two doctors, the anesthesiologist, four nurses. Liz lay on the table, conscious, her midsection numbed, a green curtain hiding the area where the incision would be made. Across the room sat two little beds, waiting.

Prompted by the nurse assigned to me, I sat in a chair next to Liz's head. We listened as the doctors bantered with each other, suggesting the twins should be named after them.

How can they joke, I wondered, *at a time like this?*

There was a long, silent moment as the doctors went to work. My breathing stopped, every muscle in my body clenching, every nerve igniting. It was as if this cold, tiled room were suddenly the vortex of the universe, as if every living thing inside and outside the building, on earth and in heaven, were straining to see what would happen.

The doctors muttered to each other. No one else moved.

All at once the anesthesiologist bent toward me. "Stand up!" he declared, and I did.

There it was — no, there *he* was! I gaped as a baby, bald and glistening, was pulled up from that rounded belly. He grimaced, not happy to be yanked into the bright light and the frigid air.

And then I heard it — the first loud cry of Christopher Morton Duckworth. It was a priceless sound, a sound Katherine had never been able to make.

Christopher grew pinker with each passing second. A nurse placed him in one of the beds as the doctors continued their work. I sat down, dazed.

Less than two minutes later the anesthesiologist signaled urgently for me to stand. Again I did, and here was another baby boy, looking exactly like his brother, right down to the grimace. The doctor grasped Jonathan David Duckworth under the arms and hauled him up, and again I heard that reassuring howl.

The doctors and nurses gathered to examine the squalling pair who kicked and wiggled in the little beds. At last we heard the words we'd waited so long to hear:

"They look just fine."

My eyes met Liz's. I could think of only one thing to say, and the tears came as I barely got it out.

"I believed I would see the goodness of the Lord in the land of the living," I said.

Her expression told me she had always believed it too.

A nurse wrapped our newborn sons in soft, white towels, elfin faces peeking out. When it was time for Liz to be wheeled to her room, the last thing she saw was her husband sitting in a chair, two tiny bundles in his arms. He was staring first at one and then the other, too happy to do anything but praise their Maker.

*   *   *   *

As I write this, the boys have just celebrated their third birthday. They're fine, and so are we.

They don't know it, but each time they toddle out the front door to ride their trikes or help me wash the car with little sponges, they pass their birth announcement on the wall. It's in needle-point, and it features Psalm 126:2-3 (NASB):

Then our mouth was filled with laughter,
And our tongue with joyful shouting;
Then they said among the nations,
"The Lord has done great things for them."
The Lord has done great things for us;
We are glad.

We're still glad, three years later.

Because sometimes the Light lasts more than just a moment.

Sometimes, by the grace of God, it's there each

morning — wanting Kix or Cheerios.
All we need are eyes to see.